SCOTTISH
ESTATE
TWEEDS

NORTH
SEA

ENGLAND

© HART 1995

TH
Tongue
Naver
Loch Naver   Wick
tnaharra
irg
Brora
Dornoch
Forres
Nairn   ELGIN
Culloden Moor   Turriff
RNESS   Spey
nadrochit   Grantown on Spey
viemore   Tomintoul
more
R.Don
Dalwhinnie   Banchory   ABERDEEN
Glenfeshie Ballater   R.Dee
Braemar   Aboyne
Blair Atholl   Laurencekirk
Pitlochry   Brechin
Kirriemuir   Montrose
Tay   Dunkeld   Forfar
Dundee
Perth
Auchterarder
EDINBURGH
Berwick on Tweed
Peebles
R.Tweed
Jedburgh

Scottish Estate Tweeds

James Johnston with his family seated in front of Newmill House, from an undated photograph probably taken early in the 1890s. Charles Johnston is on the left in the kilt. James had nine daughters and two sons. Edward Johnston, the second son, did not enter the business which passed to the Harrison family in 1920

Scottish Estate Tweeds

E P Harrison

JOHNSTONS OF ELGIN

First published in 1995 by Johnstons of Elgin
Newmill, Elgin, Morayshire IV30 2AF

Designed and produced for Johnstons of Elgin
by Atha Bellman Associates, Publishing Consultants,
Wandle Villa, 98 Phipps Bridge Road, London SW19 2ST

ISBN 0 9525329 0 5

Endpaper design by Kevin Hart

The photographs appearing on pages 23 and 26 are by Simon Pattisson ,
on pages 30, 41, 50, 58, and 87 by Heather Urquhart, ARPS
and on pages 69, 76, 84, 85 and 182-190 by Rick Beattie.
Except where a specific credit is given all the other photographs
appearing in this book are the property of
Johnstons of Elgin and are drawn
from their archives

Contents

Introduction

It is now twenty-five years since the National Association of Scottish Woollen Manufacturers published the first edition of this book then called *Our Scottish District Checks*. This work was the creation of E S Harrison, and it is appropriate that his son, also a former Chairman of Johnstons of Elgin, should be the author and compiler of this revised edition now called *Scottish Estate Tweeds*.

In 1998 Johnstons celebrate two hundred years of textile manufacturing in Elgin, no mean feat for a small Highland spinning and weaving mill in these fiercely competitive times. The history of the mill is inextricably linked both with the development of estate tweeds and also the cashmere story, which although not so important in the early days, is today a vital part of the mill's strategy.

From the estate tweeds emanated a desire to design colourful Scottish fabrics which has led the company to the forefront of European designing in woollen textiles. From the cashmere story has come a concentration on the manufacture and finishing of the soft, luxurious fabrics that world markets demand. It is therefore appropriate that this book should not just be a celebration of two hundred years, but also a record of Johnstons' history, its long association with cashmere, and an authentic documentation of the estate tweeds which now involve companies other than Johnstons.

Since 1968 when *Our Scottish District Checks* was first published many new estate tweeds have emerged, confirming that Scotland still provides inspiration for innovative textile designing. The collation of all this information has indeed been a labour of love, and were it not for Ned Harrison's persistence the record would never have been completed as far as it has. That it is, is a witness to his tenacity of purpose and knowledge of a product that is unsurpassed

Wool sorting

in the Scottish textile industry. We are, happily, in his debt. In the eighteen months that it has taken to complete this magnum opus he has been ably supported by Moira Gillespie from Johnstons and Antony Atha our publisher, both of whom deserve our grateful thanks for taking an interest in this project beyond the normal call of duty.

I hope that all of those who read this book will derive as much enjoyment from it as we have had in compiling it.

Spinning

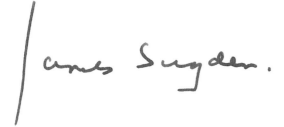

James Sugden
Managing Director
Johnstons of Elgin

Publisher's Note

The value of all transactions has been given at the price prevailing at the time remembering that before decimalisation there were 20 shillings in the £1 and 12 pence to each shilling. The 1994 values are in many cases stated in brackets after the actual figures. These equivalent prices are taken from the inflation tables supplied by the Bank of England which go back to 1270 AD and make fascinating reading.

Preface

The origins of estate tweeds are peculiarly Scottish although their use has spread far beyond the country's borders. My late father wrote *Our Scottish District Checks* in 1968 for the National Association of Scottish Woollen Manufacturers. The purpose of the book was to gather together and record an interesting group of tweeds which are part of Scottish social history before their origins were irretrievably lost. Even then, although the group was just over a hundred years old, some were already lost and the story of others was becoming third-hand memory or worse.

So the object of this edition is to try to update my father's work and add as many tweeds as possible which have been adopted since then to ensure they do not go the same way as some of the older ones. To start with we have changed the title from *Our Scottish District Checks* to *Scottish Estate Tweeds*. The term 'district check' was coined by my grandfather who was the second generation in the Edinburgh woollen merchants George Harrison & Company. Harrison's specialised in district tweeds which properly were tweeds worn by people who lived in a specific area of Scotland. These are rather different from estate tweeds and we felt that the latter title was both more accurate and easier to understand.

Nevertheless when including patterns I have stuck strictly to my father's definition which is '… a check or design (which) must belong to a particular estate and must have been used to clothe the owners and their staff.' I have therefore omitted about twenty of the patterns that appeared in the old book but which do not properly qualify under this heading.

It is only having gone through this exercise that I realise the magnitude of my father's achievement. Building on his foundations

Wool dyeing

has been time-consuming but relatively easy compared with laying the foundation, starting as he did from scratch. This has been both a fascinating and frustrating exercise; fascinating because of the wealth of new estate tweeds that came to light and the mental exploration of corners of Scotland that I had never come across; frustrating in the blank walls that met me in trying to trace the history of some of the older designs. A great many of them appear in Johnston's invoice books but just as names, without any patterns, which is most tantalising and, of course, it never says whether we were the original designers or not.

This revision would not have been possible without a great deal of outside help. I am deeply indebted to Campbells of Beauly for drawing my attention to old tweeds which had escaped my father's net and to Hunters of Brora, Haggarts of Aberfeldy, the Islay Woollen Mills and Peter MacLennan Ltd of Fort William for giving me contacts for tweeds they had made for estates since 1968. In this respect I would like to thank Mr Borland of Haggarts of Aberfeldy particularly for taking the time at the peak of his busy retail season to help me with contacts and producing patterns of tweeds for photography. Finally I must express my gratitude to all the owners of the estates who have allowed me to reproduce their tweeds in this book and supplied me with sample patterns.

Experience tells me that this account will prove to be incomplete and certainly new tweeds will be designed in the future. It should be said at this stage that all these designs and tweeds are the private property of the estate and must not be copied without their permission.

Hand spinning

Ned Harrison

Johnstons of Elgin, October 1994

The Story of Estate Tweeds

The History

The defeat of the Jacobite uprising led by Bonnie Prince Charlie at the Battle of Culloden Moor on 16th April, 1746 was a watershed in Scottish history. After Culloden Highland society changed: it changed because of military defeat; it changed through laws and legislation; it changed most of all because of economic pressure.

The origin and story of estate tweeds can be found in those changes and there is a sense in which the tweeds can be seen as a strand, albeit a very small one, of Scottish social history. To understand that history it is necessary to look at Highland society as it existed before the 1745 uprising.

Originally Highland society was tribal: it was based on a clan system which placed the chief of the clan at the apex of a pyramid. Clan chiefs occupied a semi-regal position and below them came the tacksmen, their closest kin. The chief was the main landowner and the tacksmen acted as viceroys over tracts of the chief's territories. They were also the officers in the clan regiment. They were often known by the name of the territory they held, Macdonald of Borrodale was one example, and they guarded this privilege with a fierce pride. Many tacksmen were insignificant in their poverty but some attained the status of semi-chieftains in their own domains; the Macneills of Barra who claimed the titular right to sit down to dinner before any prince on earth were tacksmen to Macdonald of the Isles and paid an annual rent of forty cows and a peregrine falcon. Some tacksmen were farmers, most were also rentiers and, like the chiefs or proprietors, they sublet land to the tenants below them. The tenants were the principal landholders and they lived together in small townships throughout the Highlands. Below these tenants were a landless class of cotters, mailers or crofters who

Opposite: The Glenfinnan monument at the head of Loch Shiel which commemorates the raising of the standard at the start of the '45 Rebellion. Photograph by Sampson Lloyd

Prince Charles Edward Stewart. 'Bonnie Prince Charlie' by an unknown artist. Reproduced by courtesy of the Scottish National Portrait Gallery

Flora MacDonald of South Uist by Richard Wilson. She was a relation of the Chief of Clanranald and was instrumental in helping Bonnie Prince Charlie to escape to France after the Battle of Culloden. She is painted in the dress of ladies of Scotland who sympathised with the Jacobite cause. Reproduced by courtesy of the Scottish National Portrait Gallery

worked for the tenants and had the right to run a cow and cultivate a small strip of land on one day a week.

Clan society was held together by the myth of a common ancestor. A typical chief was a man, most of whose clan lived upon his lands or those of his chieftains, and clan society was patriachal, involving an iron combination of duty and devotion. This duty worked both up and down. Tacksmen and tenants owed rent and service to the chief, but the chief also had an obligation to help and support those of the clan in need in times of hardship. In essence it was a military or martial society, rents were often paid in kind, and military service was a traditional form of payment. Macdonell of Keppoch, one of the two clan chiefs to be killed at Culloden, had boasted that his rent roll consisted of five hundred fighting men and military service was a payment easily enforceable where the security of land tenure depended on the goodwill of the chief or tacksman.

This pattern of life, on the face of it so timeless and unchanging was altering even as early as 1700. Sixty years had then passed since a young chief in the Western Isles had been made to lead a raid on his neighbour's lands as an initiation into manhood. The influence of the Lowlands was starting to cross the Highland line. The differences between Highlands and Lowlands based on the clan system, language (the Highlanders spoke Gaelic), religion and commercial activity were gradually being eroded but progress was infinitely slow.

After the '45 uprising the pace of this change accelerated sharply. The Jacobite rebellion had revealed the ultimate futility of the Highland appeal to arms and once that had gone there was little to stop the clan system disintegrating completely. The five thousand men raised to fight for Bonnie Prince Charlie were defeated in battle and legislation then consolidated the work of the army throughout the Highlands.

This was recognised at the time. Writing in 1787 after his Tour of the Hebrides Samuel Johnson observed:

'There was never perhaps any change of national manners so quick, so great, and so general, as that which has operated in the Highlands by the last conquest and subsequent laws. We came too late to see what we expected – a people of peculiar appearance and a system

Glen Affric in winter. Glen Affric lies to the south-west of Inverness just to the north of the Ceannacroc hills where Bonnie Prince Charlie sheltered after Culloden. Photograph by Sampson Lloyd

of antiquated life. The clans retain little now of their original character: their ferocity of temper is softened, their military ardour is extinguished, their dignity of independance is depressed, their contempt of government is subdued, and their reverence for their chiefs is abated. Of what they had before the late conquest of their country there remains only their language and their poverty.'

Culloden and its aftermath changed everything; many factors, the most important economic, came together and the old Highlands receded into a mist of romance they had done little to deserve.

One of the traditional Highland practices had been cattle stealing known euphemistically as 'lifting'. Cattle were money. The 1746

Ruthven Barracks, Kingussie. Built between 1716 and 1725 the barracks was originally intended to house a company of infantry to assist in pacifying the Highlands. It was never occupied to capacity and on the 31st August, 1745 was attacked by a force of 300 Jacobites. Sergeant Molloy and a garrison of twelve men defended the barracks successfully. Molloy was later commissioned for his bravery. Photograph by Sampson Lloyd

Act of Prohibition passed after the '45 rebellion had forbidden men and boys throughout Scotland to wear tartan and Highland clothes and also to carry arms. Cattle drovers had been exempted from this latter prohibition. When law and order was brought to the Highlands cattle stealing was eradicated and cattle ranching became a worthwhile occupation. Economic circumstances in the rest of Scotland and England in the last half of the eighteenth century changed enormously. The agricultural reforms of the late eighteenth century meant that the land could support a much larger population. Industries sprang up and created wealth and this economic expansion was probably more important than Culloden in the break up of Highland society.

Increasing prosperity manifested itself in the north as a rising demand for Highland products which in turn brought promise of material rewards to the exploiter of Highland resources on a scale without parallel.

Black cattle were the main export, and oatmeal the main import. In the fifty years between 1740–90 the price of black cattle tripled while the price of oats did not double. Furthermore the introduction of the potato as a crop that would grow on marginal land in the years after 1760 meant that far fewer oats were needed to feed the population. The potato rapidly became the staple diet of the Highlanders. At the same time the price of wool began to rise and from 1760 onwards it became appreciated that the Highlands could provide grazing grounds for the Cheviot and black-faced sheep from the south. In 1782 Sir John Lockhart-Ross became the first Highland landlord to lease grazing for sheep when he let the land at Balnagowan to Thomas Geddes, a lowland sheep farmer, and the following year Thomas Gillespie rented a sheep walk at Glen Quoich from Macdonell of Glengarry.

While black cattle could be accommodated within the traditional peasant economy of the Highlands, sheep could not. Sheep require large tracts of land on which to graze, in particular those hillsides which the Highlanders had relied on to feed their cattle each summer. The coming of the sheep led to a basic change in land tenure. Ironically the first class to suffer from the changing economic circumstances was the tacksmen, the nearest relatives of the chiefs. When the trade in black cattle expanded, chiefs found that southern graziers were prepared to pay higher rents to run their cattle on the land previously rented to the tacksmen. This brought the first emigrations. In the nineteen years between 1772–91, sixteen ships carrying some 6,400 people sailed from Inverness and Ross for Canada, Nova Scotia and America. These were orderly exits compared with the miserable departures of the next fifty years and were often organised by tacksmen themselves who took their tenants with them.

The first large clearance from the Glengarry estates in the west took place in 1785 and this was followed by large emigrations to Canada from Knoydart the following year. The first clearances in Sutherland were in 1800 where small numbers of tenants were moved from their holdings on the north of the River Oykel.

For a time the Highlands were sheltered from the harshest of the economic winds of change. The price of black cattle remained high throughout the Napoleonic wars, two industries sprang up, both of which were labour intensive and which absorbed some of the tenants who had been removed from their land, kelp farming in the Western Isles and herring fishing on the west coast and in Sutherland. There seemed grounds for optimism. The Highland

Hugh Montgomerie, Earl of Eglinton by John Singleton Copley. This flamboyant portrait shows the Earl dressed in the uniform of the Black Watch with 'Government pattern' kilt and red tunic. After Culloden the wearing of the tartan was outlawed by the 1746 Act together with the bearing of arms. Officers and soldiers in His Majesty's Forces were excepted from this and regiments recruited for the Crown wore the green, blue and black 'Government' tartan with distinguishing lines of red, white and yellow for the different regiments. The Cameron Highlanders were the first to break this convention and design their own tartan on their formation in 1793. Reproduced by courtesy of the Scottish National Portrait Gallery

Macalister. A passenger to Canada.
From The Clans of the Scottish Highlands
by R R McIan

and Agricultural Society was founded in 1784, people talked of bringing industry to the Highlands and a mill was built at Spinning-dale in Sutherland to compete with the woollen industry of York-shire and the Borders. Purpose-built villages were created at Ulla-pool and Beauly and elsewhere to promote the new herring fisher-ies and this in spite of the view held by the developers that 'the com-mon people are lazy, ignorant and addicted to drinking.'

It seemed reasonable to expect society to develop along Lowland lines where the agricultural reforms of the eighteenth century had created a class of wealthy indigenous farmers with a landless class of labourers below them and who worked for them. Lowland Scotland was generally prosperous and such development did indeed take place in some areas like Aberdeenshire, Banffshire and around Inverness. But it didn't happen in the north and west where society became dominated by large numbers of tenants holding very small parcels of land in very crowded conditions. The peasant society of the clan was replaced by a different form of peasant society based on the small holding. The tragedy of the Highlands during the first half of the nineteenth century is encapsulated within this scene.

At a time when the population was rising the economy collapsed. After 1815 cattle lost their value, the price of kelp fell from £20 a ton in 1808 to £3 a ton by 1830 when it was no longer worth gather-ing, and the herring moved from the inland lochs to the open seas where larger boats and more expensive equipment were required to harvest them. Only wool remained.

In 1792 Sir John Sinclair of Ulbster had brought the first Cheviot sheep to Sutherland. In 1795 he wrote:

'The Highlands of Scotland may sell, at present, perhaps from £200,000 to £300,000 worth of lean cattle per annum. The same ground under sheep will produce twice as much mutton, and there is wool into the bargain. If covered with the coarse-woolled breed of sheep, the wool might be worth about £300,000, the value of which can only be doubled by the art of the manufacturer; whereas the same ground under the Cheviot or True Mountain breed will pro-duce at least £900,000 of fine wool.'

The traditional Cheviot sheep of the borders had been transformed in the middle of the eighteenth century by a farmer called Robson.

Robson mated his native ewes with rams from Lincolnshire and Spain and within twenty years he created a breed of sheep which yielded a third more meat and wool and which showed considerable stamina in the harsh winters of the Highlands. Land which produced 2d an acre under cattle produced 2s under sheep.

The coming of the sheep and the economics of sheep farming spelled the end of the Highlands and made the clearances, the *cause célèbre* of Highland history, inevitable. Sir John Sinclair had pleaded with all landowners for a gradual, enlightened introduction of the Cheviot but the pace of change was too fast. Between 1807–21 between five and ten thousand people were cleared from their homes in Sutherland alone to make way for sheep and nowhere is the evidence more plainly seen than in Strathnaver.

Any tourist driving north down Loch Naver today will come, at the foot of the loch, to Achness on the hillside on the other side of the river. There the grey stones of the former houses can clearly be seen beside the cemetery, and the grass around them remains a

A border farm in the Lammermuirs. The North Country Cheviot bred by Robson in the Scottish Borders came to the Highlands at the end of the eighteenth century. Its arrival brought about the clearances. Photograph courtesy the Scottish Tourist Board

The stones of the former dwellings at Rossall in Strathnaver where Macleod was born. The top of Ben Klibreck can just be seen in the far distance. Photograph by Sampson Lloyd

brighter green, evidence of former cultivation. Three miles further down the river on the Red Brae there is a monument erected to Donald Macleod, Stonemason, author of the *History of the Destitution in Sutherlandshire* and *Gloomy Memories*. The monument stands on the left bank of the river and looks across it to the site of the former township of Rossall where Macleod was born and from where he was evicted by Patrick Sellar in June, 1814.

There is no doubt that the outrage felt at the thought of the clearances is due to Macleod. He conducted a life-long crusade against Sellar and against James Loch, the Commissioner of the Stafford Estates, and the main architect behind the 'improvements' carried out throughout Sutherland on these estates.

> 'Every imaginable means,' he wrote, 'short of the sword or the musket, was put in requisition to drive the natives away, to force them to exchange their farms and comfortable habitations, erected by themselves or their forefathers, for inhospitable rocks on the seashore, and to depend for subsistence on the watery element in its wildest mood...The country was darkened by the smoke of the burnings, and the descendants were ruined, trampled upon, dispersed and compelled.'

Thirty-five years later he wrote even more searingly of the clearances from the Western Isles:

> '... hear the sobbing, sighing and throbbing, see the confusion, hear the noise, the bitter weeping and bustle. Hear mothers and children asking fathers and husbands, where are we going? hear the reply *Chan eil fios againn* – we know not.'

With the benefit of hindsight it is necessary to see the events of the Sutherland clearances in a wider perspective. There can be no doubt that the condition of Sutherland at the beginning of the nineteenth century was primitive and backward. Stafford and Loch spent vast sums of money carrying out various schemes throughout the county in an attempt to create industry and wealth. In 1820 Loch published *An Account of the Improvements on the Estate of Sutherland belonging to the Marquess and Marchioness of Stafford*. The book contains a chronicle of his policies and catalogues the improvements made in Sutherland during the previous seven years:

half a million pounds of wool was now being exported annually; ninety miles of roads were being built; bridges were being constructed at Dornoch and Helmsdale; coal was being mined at Brora; the herring fishery at Helmsdale was established; £14,000 was invested in creating a modern port at Helmsdale alone, and so on. The list is long and impressive.

Unfortunately the pressures seen in Sutherland were common to the rest of the north and west on the Highlands. The scenes in Strathnaver were echoed in the next thirty years in Strathoykel, Glencalvie, Strathconon, Glenelg and throughout the whole of the Western Isles. Emigration was, in effect, the only answer as a growing

Looking north to the top of Loch Broom. The fishing village of Ullapool lies on the right hand side of the loch near the end of the rainbow in the picture. Loch Broom was one of the points from which the Highlanders displaced by the clearances sailed to Canada and North America at the beginning of the nineteenth century. Photograph by Sampson Lloyd

Sir Walter Scott by Sir Henry Raeburn. Scott's novels and his enthusiasm for tartans helped to promote Scotland in the early part of the nineteenth century. Reproduced by courtesy of the Scottish National Portrait Gallery

population, a decaying economy, recurrent famine – the harvest failed in 1836, potato blight came from Ireland in 1846 and the crop failed again in 1850 – and bitter poverty made exile inevitable. In 1851, following the report prepared for the Home Secretary by Sir John MacNeill, the Skye Emigration Society was founded and the Highland and Island Emigration Society was formed a year later under the patronage of Prince Albert. The clearances of the Western Isles made sure that the sheep stations in Australia and New Zealand did not lack for shepherds.

Part of the tragedy of the Highlands in the nineteenth century can be found in the first emigrations of the tacksmen in the last part of the eighteenth century. They were the people who might have formed the entrepreneurial class in society from which new ideas, new wealth and industry might have sprung. Without them there was less chance. Many of the chiefs were spendthrift and feckless. Few ploughed back any money into their estates and, when their revenues fell away, poverty and destitution forced them to sell.

The character deficiencies of these chiefs was therefore one of the reasons why estate tweeds were developed in the nineteenth century. It wasn't the only reason and there were a number of other strands which contributed to their design and creation. The first of these was the re-discovery of Scotland itself, the Scotland of the Waverley novels and Highland romance. There can be no doubt that Sir Walter Scott popularised the legend of Scotland and with it the recreation of the tartans of the clans. In the introduction to the first edition of this book, published under the title *Our Scottish District Checks* Edward Harrison wrote:

> '…it would almost be true to say that he (Scott) was, if not their only begetter, at least the creator of their modern use. The Tartans had their apotheosis in that enthusiastic fortnight in August of 1822 when George IV visited Edinburgh. Sir Walter was one of the chief hosts at the banquet in the ancient Parliament Hall at which the City entertained the King. Certainly, in the most truly glorious manner, the Tartan Cult was then launched with a flourish that probably neither before nor since has been accorded to any fashion. Certainly it resulted in one of the most truly magnificent collections of national designs ever brought together.'

Balmoral Castle, Aberdeenshire. Photograph courtesy the Scottish Tourist Board

While tartans have little in common with estate tweeds in the design sense it is certainly true that if there had been no tartans there would have been no estate tweeds.

The growing popularity of the Highlands was enormously enhanced by their adoption by Queen Victoria and Prince Albert in the middle of the nineteenth century. In 1848 Prince Albert bought the estate of Balmoral from the Farquharsons of Inverey, and the foundation stone of Balmoral Castle was laid on 28th September, 1853. One of the first things that Prince Albert did was to design *The Balmoral Tweed* for use by all the stalkers and ghillies on the estate. In spite of its name it is one of the first true estate tweeds, of a very dark blue design with white sprinkled with crimson. It gives a grey overall appearance and imitates very closely the texture and effect of the granite mountains of Aberdeenshire around Balmoral. It was designed to provide camouflage while stalking in the Aberdeenshire hills.

Many of the English aristocracy followed their monarch to

Old Mar Bridge and Lochnagar, Aberdeenshire. From a watercolour by Sutton Palmer

Scotland in the nineteenth century. Scottish estates were readily come by. Many of the Highland lairds, in particular those who lived on the West coast, wished to cut figures in society. Social life in Georgian and Regency times demanded money. Fortunes were won and lost on the gaming tables and the income from the estates was insufficient to support the dignity required of a Highland chief. Many estates were sold, some changing hands several times within thirty or forty years. The greatest sale came between 1813 and 1838 when Ranald George Macdonald of Clanranald, eighteenth captain of the clan, sold all his estates from Moidart to Arisaig on the mainland to South Uist in the Isles for £214,000. He retained only the island and castle of Tirrim. General Roderick Macneil of Barra sold his island for £42,050 in 1839 and Colonel Gordon of Cluny bought it the next year for £38,050. Mackenzie of Seaforth bought Lewis for £160,000 in 1825 and sold it twenty years later for £190,000.

Grouse shooting and deerstalking became popular and this was helped oddly enough by the increase in the importation of wool from Australia. The Cheviot sheep did not retain its profitability during the nineteenth century and many lairds found they could augment their incomes by letting the stalking and fishing on their estates to southerners. A brace of grouse was the accepted unit of value; a brace was worth 5s, and a salmon was worth twenty brace of grouse. By 1841 ninety Highland estates had shooting tenants paying £125 a month or more. The *Inverness Courier* commented that '… this new branch of trade or commerce has added greatly to the rental of many estates. Instances are not rare of the shooting letting being as high as the grazing of a mountain district.'

The literature of deerstalking also spread the popularity of the Highlands. The Sobieski Stuarts, the two imposters who gently let it be known that they were the grandsons of Bonnie Prince Charlie and were rowed down the Beauly to mass each Sunday with the Royal Standard flying at the stern of their barge, lived for several years on the island of Eilean Aigas, lent to them by Lord Lovat. There they wrote their books, *Vestiarum Scoticum* (The Costumes of the Clans), *Tales of the Century* and *Lays of the Deer Forest*, which was published in two volumes in 1848. William Scrope, neighbour of Sir Walter Scott on the Tweed, had published *Deer Stalking* ten years earlier. Landseer, Ansdell and other artists painted the Highlands

and the red deer in romantic light. Allan Gordon Cameron in *The Wild Red Deer of Scotland* wrote in poetic terms of the change from sheep to deer:

> 'Sheep-runs cleared of sheep became *ipso facto* deer-runs, and from old association were called "deer-forests", even though completely denuded of wood. …The passion for deer and the hills which had inspired the poetry of the Gael, caught fire afresh from the high tops of Athole, and at the call of Scrope, the chase of the hill stag instantaneously gripped the imagination of the sporting world.'

Stalking and salmon fishing brought wealth to the Highlands. Communications were improved. Roads and railways were built. Old lodges were refurbished. More importantly sport provided employment in the glens where:

> '…as ghillies and stalkers … dispossessed clansmen could once more pursue the sport of deer-slaying which had been the joyful recreation of their forefathers for centuries.'

As they do today deerstalking, salmon fishing and grouse shooting required professionals who could initiate the amateur into the craft of forest, moor, loch and river. Each estate had its complement of retainers and it became the custom to dress all the men of an estate in one pattern of tweed.

The Story of Estate Tweeds

The Development

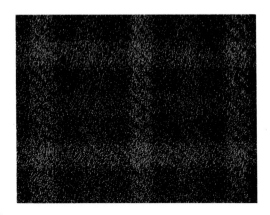

The Glen Lyon tweed. This is a District Check designed some time in the nineteenth century but the origins are unknown. It can be worn by anyone living in Glen Lyon

To some extent Estate Tweeds might be said to be distant cousins of the Clan Tartans. Both tweeds and tartans identify a group of people but while a tartan identifies members of the same family no matter where they live, estate tweeds identify people who live and work in the same area whether they are related or not.

Estate tweeds started as a Scottish phenomenon and they have spread from Scotland to other countries. They are quite modern – the first estate tweeds were created in the 1840s – but it is often surprisingly difficult to trace the origins of many of the individual patterns and the district, as opposed to estate tweeds, such as the Glen Lyon are particularly elusive in this respect. Many small mills were involved in making them although Ballantyne of Walkerburn and Johnstons of Elgin were the two main suppliers, but even at Johnstons where the main archives covering the nineteenth century have survived, only the patterns exist without comment or history. It is a pity that no one set down chapter and verse at the time.

The development of estate tweeds was largely due to the decline in the influence of the clan chiefs and landowners in the Highlands. They were seduced by the social life in Edinburgh and London but found that their estates would not support them in the style enjoyed by the southern aristocracy. At the same time they found many anxious to follow the example of Queen Victoria and Prince Albert and own or rent a sporting estate or deer forest.

One of the old traditions of the Highlands had been the provision by the chiefs of clothing for their retainers in the clan tartan. New tenants and owners wanted to follow this example but had no right to wear a tartan. The first estate tweed, the Glenfeshie, is a good illustration of this. Between 1834 and 1841 the estate of Glenfeshie which belonged to Sir George MacPherson-Grant was rented by General Balfour of Balbirnie and the Rt Hon Edward Ellice MP. Miss Balfour, the General's daughter in the words of her son, was:

> '...disturbed because she had no tartan so she designed the check which Mr Ellice and the ghillies and keepers all wore from that day to the present.'

The design was a simple variant of the Shepherd Check. Around 1770, Campbell of Combie brought John Tod up from Dumbarton to tend his sheep. Later a second shepherd, Braidfoot, brought another lot of Cheviots north. Border shepherds wore the traditional shepherd's plaid, a little black and white check made up with about six threads of black and six of white. Miss Balfour varied this pattern by superimposing a scarlet overcheck which gave her a 'tartan' for her staff. History has it that she adopted this design because the colours imitated the grey and red granites of the mountains around Glenfeshie but it seems more likely that she changed the design to distinguish the men of the forest from the shepherds.

A secondary reason for the creation of estate tweeds was the need to provide a camouflage for the stalkers when they were on the hill. To look at the Glenfeshie, the Coigach or the Dacre might appear to do the opposite but it is surprising how effective many of the brightest tweeds are at breaking up a man's outline on the hill. In most cases the colours chosen were those which blended well with the background of mountain and moor in an area. There is a good example of this in the choice of tweed for Strathconon. Mr Peter Combe, whose family used to own the estate, found among his grandfather's effects a group of patterns, eight variations on the old Strathconon tweed. He said that these patterns dated from the time when his grandfather was experimenting with the weaver to find the most suitable blend for the hill. The eight variations were produced and the stalkers were sent up the hill with sample lengths while his grandfather sat on the front porch of the lodge with his glass to see which tweed was the most invisible. The late Lord Lovat too related how his grandfather had pointed out to his wife that the colours on the far shore of Loch Morar, sands, heather, bracken, bluebells and birches blended together to make one beautiful colour effect. And from this blend was created the original Lovat mixture.

A border shepherd wearing the traditional black and white plaid used to wrap lambs. From a photograph taken about 1900. Reproduced by courtesy the National Museum of Scotland

The effectiveness of estate tweeds as a camou-flage on the hill is clearly shown in this photo-graph. While the pony is prominent the pony man is almost invisible lying in the rocks

Broadly speaking, the designs used in estate tweeds fall into four groups. The first group follows the example set by Miss Balfour and uses variations on the Shepherd Check (page 173) and this includes those designs which are based on the Coigach (page 110) and which are known throughout the world as 'gun clubs'. The second uses variations of the Glenurquhart (page 139). The third is based on tartan-type designs while the fourth uses a number of plain grounds with or without overchecks and form the group from which camouflage uniform evolved.

In the first group the Glenfeshie (page 88) is the simplest design but many of the tweeds vary the colour of the black and white as well as introducing overchecks. The gun club designs are an adaptation of the Shepherd where the white ground is retained but the black is alternated with another colour. The Coigach was probably the first design to do this and around 1870 this design was adopted by one of the American Gun Clubs, either New York or Baltimore no-one knows which, as their club colours. The style was then re-exported back to Britain from America and became known throughout the fashion world as a gun club.

The Glenurquhart design from which the second group of estate tweeds comes is possibly the most famous contribution made by the Scottish tweed industry to the fashion world. The original design was adopted by Caroline, Countess of Seafield for her estate at Glen Urquhart. Lady Seafield was herself a handloom-weaver and has been credited with the design but it is more likely that it was created by Elizabeth Macdougall who lived at Lewiston, a little village at the foot of the glen where it opens out to Loch Ness. William Fraser the local weaver who was to weave the cloth could not understand Elizabeth's instructions so she scratched the pattern on the ground at his cottage door with a stick. The pattern itself is a derivative of the Shepherd and is made up of blocks of small checks, usually four threads of white and four of a colour, alternated with a stripe effect of two and two in the same colours. The original Glenurquhart was woven in dark navy-blue and white but this was later changed to black and white.

The third group of estate tweed designs had no particular feature but the last group are based on a plain ground, sometimes made with marled yarn where two or more colours are twisted together before weaving, but more usually based on a mixture where wools dyed to different shades are mixed before spinning to blend into one colour. Often these designs have overchecks.

The original mixture was no doubt the Lovat (page 162) which was first made and woven by Johnstons of Elgin on 26th September, 1845 for Macdougalls of Inverness and invoiced as 'Lord Lovat's Mixture'. The story behind the creation of Lovat tweed is told in detail in the section on individual tweeds but it is worth noting that this coincided with the development of the Hodden Grey tweed designed by Lord Elcho. He was raising the London Scottish Regiment at the time and thought it wrong that soldiers should be clad in so conspicuous a colour as scarlet. Lord Elcho clothed his regiment in a cloth which blended white and claret-brown, which produced an effect similar to the red-brown soil of East Lothian. This cloth which is now more usually known as the Elcho mixture was the origin of the khaki worn by the British army and thus Lord Elcho can claim his uniform as the beginning of all the camouflage uniforms of the armies of the world.

In estate tweeds the actual colours used are important and should be matched as closely as possible. In this they differ from tartans where all colour variations are acceptable so long as they conform to the basic colour laid down. For instance green can be a light or dark

Sinclair. A Highland girl wearing a shawl or arisaid of tartan. The snood means she is unmarried. From The Clans of the Scottish Highlands *by R R McIan*

North Country Cheviot sheep near Lecht in the Scottish Highlands. Photograph by Sampson Lloyd

shade or any variation. However it is becoming increasingly difficult to match the original colours as most estate tweeds rely on one or more mixture yarns for their effect. Mixtures are more trouble and more costly to produce than single colour yarns. They require the mill to hold stocks of various colours of wool and this used to be common practice in the first half of this century when most Scottish mills would accept an order for a single fifty yard piece of cloth.

In the last thirty years the rise in the cost of finance and the introduction of high speed production machinery means that most mills ask for a minimum order for two or three pieces of cloth (one hundred and twenty to one hundred and eighty metres) and they have also reduced the number of mixtures that they carry in their yarn strings. For instance Johnstons of Elgin used to carry about forty mixtures in stock in the early 1950s now they carry ten. Any estate therefore wanting to copy the old tweed might have to bear a considerable financing cost. Nevertheless it is still possible to make up patterns of the old estate tweeds and the creation of over a hundred new tweeds since the first edition of this book in 1968 shows this is still a thriving industry. The main companies in this field now are Haggarts of Aberfeldy, Hunters of Brora and the Islay Woollen Mills.

One thing would not be possible to emulate nowadays without the artifice of dyeing. Several of the old designs were made with what was known as 'laid whites' for example the Green Mar. Laid whites came from sheep which had been anointed with a mixture of tar and tallow or butter to protect them and their wool supposedly from the severity of the winter weather. Not surprisingly the mixture always stained the wool to a deep cream shade and the fleeces were marketed as 'laid'. Instructions on the treatment of sheep with tar and tallow can be found in John Luccock's *Essay on Wool*, 1809 and Bakewell's *Observations on Wool*, 1808.

The practice was abandoned in England and the Borders quite early on and therefore the patterns based on the Shepherd Check used a pure white while those of purely Highland origin did not necessarily do so. Many of the colours have changed over the years as a number of the designs are now nearly a hundred and fifty years old. Traditionally the dye used was based on vegetable matter and small lots were dyed in a variety of shades without any constant quality control. Nowadays this is not so and the chemical dyes produce a constant colour. The laid fleeces were awkward to work and much of the weight of the fleece was lost in scouring. There is a verse in an old Scottish ballad which mentions this difficulty.

Tarry'oo, tarry 'oo,
Tarry 'oo is ill to spin:
Caird it weel, caird it weel,
Caird it weel or ye begin.
When it's cairded, rowed and spun,
Then the wark is halflins dune;
When it's woven, dressed and clean,
It micht be cleidith for a Queen.

'oo = wool, *ill* = difficult, *caird* = card, *wark* = work, *cleidith* = cloth

The Story of
Johnstons of Elgin

The Early Years
1797 – 1850

The history of Johnstons of Elgin is long and proud. The company has traded for nearly two hundred years from its present site at Newmill on the banks of the River Lossie and in all that time has been owned and run by just two families, the Johnstons and the Harrisons. Today the name of Johnstons is synonymous with cloth of the highest quality. As far back as 1851 the company pioneered the weaving of vicuna and cashmere in Scotland and these luxury fibres remain the foundation of the company's products and success as the twenty-first century approaches.

Johnstons was founded by Alexander Johnston in the last years of the eighteenth century although the exact date remains uncertain. A memorial tablet to him in the graveyard at Elgin Cathedral states that he was born on 31st December, 1774 at Ardiffray in the parish of Cruden, Aberdeenshire and history has it that he originally came to Elgin to manage the Bleachfield at Deanshaugh. According to Young's *Annals of Elgin*, published in 1878:

> 'In the end of the last century Messrs Robertson and Forsyth had a small woollen manufactory in a close a little to the east of Lossie Wynd. They were succeeded by the late Mr Alexander Johnston who appears to have removed to Newmill as early as 1800 having taken a lease from Mr King, the then proprietor of the mills. In a memorial laid before the (Town) Council on 4th December, 1800, Mr Johnston stated that he had lately erected an engine for scrubbing (scribbling) and carding of wool with slobbing and spinning jennies for the manufacture of woollen yarn.'

Alexander asked the Town Council to request the Board of Trustees for Manufactures to make him a grant which they were very willing

Opposite: The Cathedral, Elgin. The ruins are on the opposite bank of the River Lossie to Johnston's mill and the photograph was taken near the intake sluice to the old mill lade. The cathedral, one of the most beautiful in Scotland, was started in 1224, and was ransacked and burnt by the notorious Wolf of Badenoch at the end of the fourteenth century

to do. Payment of this grant, however, must have been subject to bureaucratic delays as the £100 (£2837) did not appear in the company's books until 19th December, 1807.

The original records of Johnstons of Elgin have survived and from them we learn that Alexander Johnston's main business was linen and flax with a substantial input from tobacco and oatmeal. Oatmeal, a local crop, was ground at Newmill Meal mill, which was one of the five neighbouring mills which relied on the River Lossie for power. The oats came from Newmill Farm and another farm some three miles south of Elgin called Level which was leased by Alexander Johnston for a time.

On the first page of the first book entitled *Day Book and Journal* there are references, amongst others, to Bleachfield and the farm of Level. The Bleachfield entries in the book refer to the purchase, preparation and spinning of flax, selling the yarn and possibly some cloth weaving as well. On 15th March, 1800 an entry in the invoice book records the shipment of '60 matts' (about 1,900 lbs) of flax from Rotterdam followed by another 50 matts the following month from J. van Edmont & Sons on a ship captained by Gehrt Hendrik Kuyper. The majority of flax used by the mill was purchased locally from Robert Knight of Portsoy who may have imported it himself as it is described as 'Dutch'.

An interesting item on the first page of the *Day Book* refers to Alexander Johnston's salary – £80 for the year 28th October, 1797 to 20th October, 1798. The amount (just over £2300 at today's values) does not seem large.

In August 1801 there is the first reference to a 'wool' account. On 1st December of that year there is a reference to 'carding' wool and on 31st December and 25th January the following year there are two entries to a John Grigor per 'sorting wool and washing wool.' It would seem from the *Day Book* that the linen business was phased out during the first decade of the nineteenth century and the woollen side phased in. There is a mention of a carding engine in the accounts for 1800 although this could just as well have been for linen as wool. There are further references to carding engines in the early 1800s and in 1802 and 1804 there are specific references to carding machines at Ballindalloch and Grantown. It may have been that Alexander carded wool at those two establishments

Elgin   *Anno* 1798

October 15th

November 5th

December 7th

The first page of the first Day Book and Journal dated 1798. The entries for the two farms and Bleachfield are clearly listed in the beautiful script of the period

leaving Newmill and Bleachfield for linen manufacture. What is certain is that in 1808 there is an invoice for a pair of fulling stocks, on 23rd December, 1808 there is an invoice for teazles and on 10th January, 1810 there is an invoice for broad and narrow loom shuttles. The wool side was therefore firmly established by 1810 although the rent for the Bleachfield continued to be paid up to 8th February, 1813.

Alexander Johnston seems to have had three partners in the early years. The first was William Morrison. An entry in the Ledger notes 'Nov 9 1799 to Wm Morrison £251:12:10.' An account existed in Morrison's name until 1st September, 1802 when it was closed without any further information on him.

On the 5th October, 1807 there is an entry 'William Sim for his share of stock £2000.' It would appear that William Sim became a partner, certainly £2000 (£56,750) was a substantial sum of money to invest at that time, and there are references in the next few years to the firm of Johnston and Sim, but in November 1812 Johnston wrote to John Anderson of the Leithwalk Foundry in Edinburgh:

'I hold five shares of the Hercules Insurance Company. Could you sell them for me at £14 or £15. W. Sim is now out of the business and I need all the cash I can muster.'

It looks as if he had to buy him out.

The final venture into outside partnerships came in 1829 when Alexander wrote to Douglas Edwards his agent in Aberdeen:

'I have also in view taking a Brother-in-law into my business as a partner (this however you may keep to yourself) & at present do not wish to pledge myself to any particular arrangement.'

The brother-in-law, William McAndrew, did join as a junior partner on a one-third basis and for a time the firm was known as Johnston and McAndrew but three years later he was gone and on 20th October, 1832 Alexander wrote to a customer:

'You will observe that the firm is altered to my name my late partner having left, in consequence of the business not paying to his expectations.'

After that the firm was known by its original name of Alexander Johnston until 1838 when Alexander's son James joined him as a partner and the title became Alexander Johnston & Son. When Alexander retired in 1846 the firm became James Johnston and when James took his own son, Charles, into partnership in 1868 it became James Johnston & Co and it remained James Johnston & Co until the 1940s.

It would appear that Alexander Johnston had a considerable struggle to establish his business and also that he was prepared to turn his hand to a number of ventures. The first two Johnstons were tough, determined entrepreneurs and the history of the company in the early years makes fascinating reading as in many ways it echoes the fortunes of the north of Scotland during the first half of the nineteenth century; the ventures into the herring trade and the comments on the establishment of weaving manufacturing in Sutherland are particular examples of this.

Apart from the linen trade Alexander Johnston dabbled initially in tobacco and snuff, the sale of hats – he purchased twelve boxes of hats from Philip Wood & Co of Manchester in January 1813 for £250:10:0 (£5350) – and herrings. The hat business was abandoned in 1814 when he wrote to the suppliers:

'We do not find that doing your business corresponds with our own therefore as soon as possible shall settle the different accounts.'

He succeeded in covering his costs on this venture but the same could not be said of the herring sales which came to grief badly.

His first venture into this trade had been in August 1813 when he was involved in a barter deal with Robert Finlayson of Lybster. There is no further mention of herrings until October 1818 when a letter records the sale of 130 barrels at 30s a barrel and a remark that 400 barrels had been sold to a Mr Forbes of Aberdeen. But the next year sales went badly and on 7th December he wrote to Farquhar and Morris, the London agents thanking them for their efforts on his behalf in '...the Herring Transaction which has been an unfortunate one to all concerned.' He tried again in the autumn of 1820 but the trade failed and after that he abandoned herrings altogether. His experience mirrored the fortunes of the Highlands in this industry which at that time, proved so ephemeral.

Alexander's speculations were entered in the Ledger under the attractive title 'Adventure in....' There was one adventure in wood

Drawing of a herring girl by Charles St John, the famous Scottish naturalist and writer who lived at South College in Elgin. In 1848 St John wrote that 'the supply of herring does not seem to be nearly so regular or so much to be depended on as formerly; and frequently the men are but badly paid for their expense and risk'

with a Mr William Young which cost him £17:17:3 and another in 'Militia Insurance' with an Elgin lawyer which showed a profit. He sent some woollens on consignment to Halifax, Nova Scotia in June 1813 (Johnstons' first attempt to export) which made a loss of £19:11:6 and in 1815 there was a single shipment to Jamaica of eight short pieces of 'blues' valued at £92. These were for one Alexander Barclay. The order was fulfilled and paid for. No patterns have survived of the early cloths but in the Galashiels idiom 'blues' are good solid cloths, well milled or felted, such as would be used by seafarers.

The Johnstons also held shares in a number of coasters. In the early years of the nineteenth century transport in northern Scotland was still fairly rudimentary. There was no public transport north of Aberdeen and such mail as there was was carried by horseback on three days each week. Consequently nearly all goods were transported by sea using the local harbours of Burghead, Nairn, Lossiemouth, Buckie and Inverness. The Johnstons may have

An artist's impression of Nairn Harbour, 1880.
From the engraving by George Reid RSA

Nairn. 1880.

Old Lossiemouth. From a painting by Emma Black

bought shares in some coasters so that they could get priority in shipping their goods, or, more probably, because they wanted to take part in what appears to have been a lucrative trade. There were several of these although the Ledger is not clear whether the vessels existed at the same time or whether they succeeded each other. The first mention is as early as 1799 when there is an entry in the combined *Day Book and Journal* on the 30th March:

> 'Bought of Mr A Allan (an Elgin solicitor) one eighth of the Brigantine *Marquis of Huntly of Spey* of date the 14th inst for which have received his letter of Trust. Amount £75(£1900).'

On 21st February, 1803 Alexander seems to have invested in the sloops *Eliza* and *Elizabeth* of the Leith Shipping Company. On 29th June, 1813 there is the record of a dividend of £50 being paid from the sloop *Farmer* and on the 14th September the same year, Alexander received another £50 being his share of the sale of the *Farmer*. The Journal for 1st March, 1834 shows a dividend of £14 being paid on account of the schooner *Speedwell*, half of which he paid to his partner William McAndrew.

James Johnston followed his father into shipping as the Ledger of 1845 shows he had a share in the Burghead schooner *Favourite* while in a letter to a W F Anderson in 1853 he enclosed '...receipt of my share in the *Isabella Napier*' although whether this meant he was selling his share or not is not clear.

The harbour, Burghead. From a painting by Emma Black

The first mail coach from Aberdeen to Inverness did not start until 1812 and that was succeeded by a private service in a coach called *The Duke of Gordon* which left Aberdeen at 6am and reached Inverness at 10pm. Gradually the coach service improved and there are many invoices in the ledgers indicating despatch via *The Star, The Defiance* or *The Earl of Fife*, the names of some of the earliest coaches. These despatches were for direct deliveries to the smaller local customers. Goods for the south went by coach or, if bulky, by sea to Aberdeen for trans-shipment to Edinburgh or London. Eventually everything went by rail but before the completion of the line to Inverness there was a half-way stage when goods were still sent by sea to Aberdeen to the railhead there for onward despatch.

For all the 'adventures' and speculations, weaving and woollen goods became the main part of the business. From the earliest days Alexander seems to have travelled widely seeking markets for his goods and he augmented the firm's turnover by selling cloth from other manufacturers and also by acting as agent, weaving and making up wool for the local farmers. As early as 30th April, 1803 the *Day Book and Journal* records an entry of £18:2:6 for 'London expenses' and on 21st July the same year there is another entry for expenses of £7:11:6 for a visit to Glasgow. By the end of the first thirteen years the *Day Book* records sales over the length and breadth of Scotland, from Wick in the North down to the Borders and from Montrose in the East to Campbeltown in the West.

To start with the sales were fairly small and were mainly to small tailors, individuals also bought direct from the mill and these ranged from Murdoch the shoemaker who bought '1½ of Blue & white check and 1¾ Brown Tweel' for 5s:1p in May 1844 to the Duke of Richmond and Gordon who bought '71½ yards G.T. (Gordon Tartan) @ 5s:3p a yard' in July the same year.

Towards the end of the 1830s some larger accounts began to appear in the cities of London, Glasgow and Edinburgh and gradually the balance of trade changed towards fewer accounts. A jotter belonging to James Johnston records; '*Patterns taken by Father to London on 10th May, 1841*' and two years later there is a similar entry; '*Patterns given Father to show in London 8th April, 1843.*' In each case there is a list of fifteen or so patterns with prices against each one. While these patterns have not survived they could perhaps be the predecessors of the estate tweeds which were created by the firm during the second half of the nineteenth century.

James Johnston joined his father in the business in 1835. The first time his name appears in the Journal is on 30th May of that year, 'To James Johnston for one year's salary £30' and two years later an entry on 11th August records:

'Stock Dr to James Johnston for present from his Father on his Twenty-first Birthday £100.'

By 1837 he was a partner drawing a third of the profits.

As a result of the determination of Alexander Johnston the firm not only survived, it prospered. The turnover figures for many of the early years are available and they tell a story of fluctuations in trade which mirror the fortunes of the Highlands in the early part of the nineteenth century. In 1808 the first year for which there are figures the turnover was £2,400 (£65,520) and this rose rapidly throughout the Napoleonic Wars to a peak of £6,040 (£148,160) in 1814. Thereafter the turnover declined sharply to £3,230 (£85,000) in 1817 but after that date it started to rise again. The source of the figures then dries up for over a decade and the only statistic recorded is the consumption of wool which rose throughout the 1820s from around 27,500 lbs at the start of the decade to about 45,000 lbs at the end. After that date there was another decline and wool consumption dropped to a low of 37,000 lbs in 1835.

In spite of these fluctuations by the end of the 1820s Alexander was confident enough to seek security of tenure on the mill at Newmill. On 21st November, 1827 he wrote to Robert Bain of Elgin (his landlord's lawyer) with a view to getting a feu, (a lease in perpetuity) from his landlord, Captain Stewart of Lesmurdie. He offered a lump sum of £1000 (£32,160) for the buildings and an annual feu duty of £40. Nothing came of this offer and in 1830 he wrote again directly to Captain Stewart.

In his letter he stated his intention to make:

'…a considerable addition to our manufacturing establishment in the course of the summer and our lease being now so far run you may suppose it is with reluctance that we lay out more money on buildings here on such an uncertainty.'

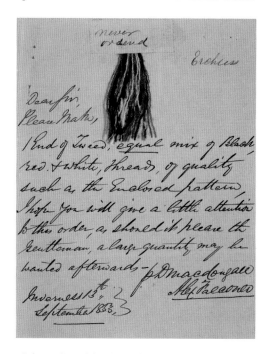

A letter from Macdougalls of Inverness asking for a sample piece of tweed to be made up. Erchless is written at the top of the letter but the design is nothing like the Erchless tweed and the label 'never ordered' shows that the order was abandoned

Alexander implied that if he did not get his feu he would have to move to premises at Deanshaugh which he had been offered. In a second letter to Captain Stewart written on 9th February, 1831 he reminded Captain Stewart that:

'... it is very improbable you will find any tenant or tenants disposed to pay you so high a rent as we do now, as the premises are laid out in such a manner as to be ill calculated for anything except a manufactory, and the recent extensive failures and present universal depression in this branch of commerce are as you must be well aware more than sufficient to damp effectually the ardor of the most sanguine speculator.'

It would seem likely that some arrangement was arrived at around that time although there is no record of any in the Ledger. The feu was finally granted on 19th May, 1836. when it appears in the ledger without comment for the lump sum of £1000 and an annual feu duty of £50 but by then a fair degree of building had taken place not just at the factory where the waterwheel was incorporated in a new building but by the construction of a row of houses in Collie Street about half a mile from the mill which started at the end of 1829. These houses have since become known most appropriately as 'Shuttle Row'. It is doubtful if Alexander would have undertaken this expenditure unless he had sufficient security.

During the nineteenth century there were a number of small mills working in the North and of them only Newmill and the little mill at Knockando have survived, bankruptcies were common and this would have lent strength to Alexander's argument. One thing which has survived is a letter written on 10th February, 1849 by James Johnston to George Gunn who was agent or factor to the Duke of Sutherland. It is worth quoting in full for it underlines the state of the Highlands and the difficulties that beset manufacturing industry in the North.

'I beg to acknowledge your favour of the 7th suggesting to me the establishing a Woollen Manufactory in Sutherlandshire. A similar suggestion, I believe, was made to my Father by the late Duchess of Sutherland some 40 years ago, which he declined and I fear things are not altered so much as to induce me now to adopt it.

The building which was erected in 1847 as a wool drying house and store. The brick-work on the first floor windows was probably added when the wooden louvres of the dry-ing floor were replaced. Part of the old records of the company were discovered in the attic space at the top of the building. It is now part of the shop and visitor's centre

The oldest buildings on the mill site are the building to the right of the present office and reception area, (see page 69) which was once part of the weaving shed and was powered by one of the two water wheels, and the tower building behind it. The office was a house up until 1860 and the porch and the mansard roof were added later. The other old buildings are the cottages on the left at the entrance to the mill which were created from the old farm buildings

Such a work I have no doubt would be a convenience in the County and also be of much use in giving employment etc. tho' perhaps in the last respect not to the extent the worthy Duke may expect as at first probably three fourths of the workers would have to be brought from a distance, and it would take years to break in and teach your labourers many of the processes — this of course would be a serious expense and drawback and the want of competent mechanics to make and mend things constantly required, would be still more felt. All experience shows that Goods can be made more cheaply and Business conducted with far less capital in a Manufacturing district where every requirement is at hand, than where the Mill is isolated in a remote rural quarter — the being near the raw material is of very little consequence and in Sutherlandshire (where farmers ship off their wool immediately on consignment to Liverpool if unsold on the market) would be more than counterbalanced by being obliged to lay in 12 months supply at once, or not getting it when required.

I fear the local demand of the Manufactured article would be but limited — at least that is my experience in this quarter where I feel sadly my distance from the Southern markets to which I send most of my goods.

If the Duke of Sutherland is really anxious to have a mill set agoing in his County I fear he must offer strong inducements to counterbalance all these disadvantages and before thinking of the thing at all, I should like to have some idea of what these may be and also his views as to extent etc. Meanwhile with kind regards I remain.'

Writing to his lawyer fifteen years later in response to a request to assist a client setting up a mill at Kingussie, Johnston said:

'My father commenced here in much this way upwards of 60 years ago and by degrees the place has increased considerably, but it has been an uphill work compared with what others have had in the Manufacturing districts and what I would not recommend others to undertake.'

Taken in conjunction with the Spinningdale venture of the 1780s these letters give a fascinating insight into the difficulties that the Johnstons must have faced in their early years.

It is possible to surmise that the willingness shown by the first two Johnstons to experiment, to try anything once was their greatest strength. There were occasions when these experiments went very awry. The Letter Book tells of a disastrous scheme to spin worsted yarn for the handknitting trade in 1836. Alexander appears to have entered the plan with a Mr D Popplewell of Aberdeen and the idea seems to have been for Johnstons to manufacture the yarn which Popplewell was going to sell. A year later Alexander wrote to Popplewell saying:

'the yarn hitherto made is at a dead loss and I must confess I do not at present see very clearly how it will ever be otherwise with the small quantity we can make.'

Dunrobin Castle, Sutherland from the sea. The castle is the seat of the Earls of Sutherland and has been inhabited since the thirteenth century. The oldest part of the castle is on the extreme left and the centre section was rebuilt by the Duchess Countess in 1785. The romantic right hand section is the work of Sir James Barry, architect of the Houses of Parliament, who was employed by the 2nd Duke between 1845–50. Elizabeth, the Duchess Countess married George Leveson-Gower, 2nd Marquess of Stafford, later 1st Duke of Sutherland. It was his 'improvements' throughout Sutherland which contributed to the clearances. Photograph by Sampson Lloyd

Dallas Moor and Ben Rinnes. From a painting by Emma Black. The village of Dallas just south-west of Elgin has given its name to the great American city in Texas. There was a small weaving mill there in the nineteenth century and in 1856 James Johnston sold two old power looms to the manager William Peat, who had been a former Johnstons' employee. The price was 10 guineas and the credit terms were a generous twelve months

In August that year there is a journal entry showing a loss of £355 (£12,500).

Another venture which caused considerable trouble was an order from the Rifle Brigade at Windsor in 1840. On 21st January Alexander acknowledged the order from Colonel Brown:

'We had duly your favor of 11th inst. I am obliged for your order for trowser stuff for your men. We have today got the patterns referred to from Sergeant Fraser and shall get the quantity required for the privates, say 2,230 yards, made up in the course of the spring and the summer – paying attention to your remarks as to exact conformity to pattern in fabric and colour.'

But the order was so large that it overstretched Alexander's production capacity. Part of the order was subcontracted, firstly to Benjamin Gott of Leeds and then to J & W Archibald of Menstrie near Stirling. The Colonel complained about the colour and quality, credit was demanded. Alexander wrote in plaintive terms:

'As to the price of the cloth we are quite at your mercy and if you think 5s: 6p sufficient we must sacrifice all our profit – considering the Credit not an out of the way one and submit to it.'

Undaunted in November he was writing to Colonel Brown again seeking an order for officer's cloth.

Glen Nevis in winter. Ben Nevis, the highest mountain in Scotland lies out of the picture on the left. Photograph by Sampson Lloyd

The output of the firm was diverse and seems to have moved from the simplest to the most sophisticated. In the early years there are a lot of references to blues and serges both of which are traditional hard wearing cloths. Gradually however new cloths came in. Johnstons started to make angolas, a cloth with a cotton warp and woollen weft, which sold well for many years, (eight pieces of Cheviot and cotton tweed were shipped to Phipps and Stewart of New York as late as July, 1893) and the firm also sold large quantities of a cloth called Orleans, better known as umbrella cloth, for at one time it was used in the manufacture of umbrellas.

Until the middle of the nineteenth century the bulk of the sales was made from stock patterns but this changed as more merchants wanted to sell patterns exclusive to them. The reputation that Johnstons acquired in the manufacture of the district or estate tweeds helped their sales in this respect and they benefited from the patronage of Lord Lovat. Newmill wove the first piece of Lovat mixture which has since become part of the woollen trade's vocabulary. The pattern books which start in 1853 and run through to 1960 show a variety of cloths from heavy to medium in weight and a variety of finishes. The patterns vary from the sombre-coloured ones to the lighter ones of the estate tweed type.

Another speciality in the early years was the manufacture of the traditional Scottish plaid sometimes called a maud. A plaid is a piece of cloth 'six quarter' (fifty-four inches) wide and about five yards long. They were no doubt much used by travellers in the stage coaches of the first part of the century but as travel by rail and then motor car came in smaller travelling rugs became more popular and the sale of plaids declined. Plaids were sold abroad as well as in the home market and there is an amusing exchange between James Johnston and Sanderson Brothers of Durban in 1850 when, after an encouraging reply to James's query as to whether plaids would sell in Natal, a case of plaids was shipped. On 5th April, 1852 James wrote to Mr Allan C. Gow his agent in Glasgow:

'Sir. Mr Sanderson has returned the parcel of plaids he recommended me sending to Port Natal six months ago. They cost me some £10 of expenses and the customs house in London where they now lie, is inclined to give some trouble besides. I shall be obliged

An order from Macdougalls of Inverness for Lovat tweed dated April, 1852. It is noticeable how the shade varied from time to time and different quality was required for the keepers on the estate

Dear Sir,

I have just seen Lord Lovat who has fixed on the mixed wool without the gray, and seems quite delighted with the shade, so that you will please get on with the under noted order without the least delay – Send me patterns of all the Lovat tweed on hand & making, as I may soon dispose of them.

I am, Dear Sir, your truly

Inverness 2nd April 1852

3 pcs fine Lovat Tweed same quality as last
3 " heavy make such as this pattern in substance for his Keepers
1 " good quality substance such as this but without the finish on the face closely woven – not rough, for his own use

All the above six pieces to be made same Color as this sample of wool enclosed here – but not darker

3 plaid same shade

by your signing the enclosed declaration before a magistrate, it being required with a similar one from myself before they can be cleared free of duty.'

To add insult to injury three plaids were stolen in the customs house and the concluding sentence of James's letter to Sanderson says with some justification 'I am certainly not likely to try further consignments to your quarter.'

The decade 1840–50 was an important one for the firm. The

turnover in 1840 was £4,100 (£129,000) having been as high as £4,560 (£178,340) in 1835 but by 1849 it had risen to £7,350 (£287, 450). In 1845 Alexander retired (he died in 1864, aged ninety) and in July 1847 James wrote to John Smith the Edinburgh printer asking for a hundred and forty copies of the following circular:

Newmill, Elgin 1st July, 1846
'My father having twelve months ago ceased to be a partner in the firm of "Alex^r Johnston & Son" and retired altogether from the business here in my favor, I intend after this date to carry it on in my own name. Soliciting a continuance of your favours which shall at all times have my best attention. I am etc.'

During this period James started experimenting with the more exotic wools on which the reputation of the company is now based. On 8th March, 1842 he bought some alpaca from W & B Newsome which was used in a blend with wool. Presumably it was used to improve the handle, 'the feel', of the cloth and it was not until seven years later that we read of fifteen yards of alpaca cloth being sent to Thomas Smith of Inverness on 21st September. Thereafter sale of alpaca cloth became quite common. On 23rd January, 1849 James wrote to John Hume of Glasgow, a wool importer:

'The Peru wool arrived two days ago....Is there any vicuna wool in

The first ledger entry for vicuna dated 2nd February, 1849. Purchases of vicuna rose steadily throughout the 1850s and '60s to a peak of 5400lbs in 1865 when the price had dropped to 3s per pound. Thereafter the use of vicuna declined as the price rose

your market? If so I shall be obliged by your sending me a small sample with price.'

A sample must have been in stock for a week later James wrote:

'I am in receipt of your of 27th with sample of Vicuna Wool. It appears coarser to me than I expected and before ordering a large quantity I should like to try a sample Ballot.'

A ballot was a small bale and, as in those days the fleece could only be obtained by killing the wild vicunas which was illegal, history has it that it was smuggled out of the producing countries inside larger bales of alpaca. Whether this story is correct or not it always arrived in small bags. On 2nd February the ballot arrived weighing sixty-one pounds at 5s:6p(£10) a pound. This was an exorbitant price for raw fibre and when he settled the account on 28th March James wrote pessimistically to Hume:

'It turned out much coarser than I expected and was more difficult to work so that I shall lose money by it and not likely to try more.'

Whatever the prognostication, the yarn was woven on 11th April by Peter Kynoch, a weaver of great experience, into eight plaids and twelve shawls. These were invoiced in July to Macdougalls of Inverness at two and a half times the price of ordinary Shepherd plaids as Super Vicuna and Macdougalls sold all of them within two months. Macdougalls seems to have been involved in the enterprise from the beginning as James had written earlier:

'...am making enquiry in Leeds if I can get the wool spun there in which case I could make you whatever you want of it...'

Another important customer who placed his first order in July, 1841 was James Locke of 119 Regent Street, London. Locke was a famous name in the wool trade and probably did more than any other merchant to popularise Scottish cloths in the South. He is usually credited with the origin of the word 'tweed'. The story goes that Watsons of Hawick invoiced some *tweel* (which was the standard name for Scottish cloth because of its twilled appearance) but the word was written carelessly and was read as 'tweed'. The association with the famous Border river made the mistake a natural one and the name stuck.

A letter from James Locke requesting a contribution to the Christmas box for his employees. This was a customary practice in the woollen trade and contained the implied threat of 'No contribution, no orders next year'

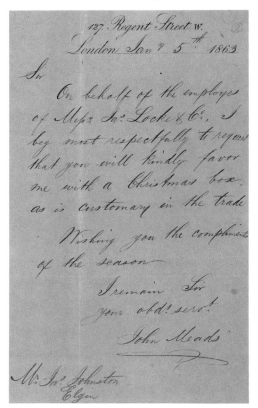

The Brewery Bridge over the River Lossie at Newmill. In the nineteenth century when the weir in the foreground was breached either for repairs to the bridge or the weir the power source for the mill was cut off and all work stopped. To keep the workers quiet they were then provided with free porter

The weir slants towards the intake sluice for the lade which is just off the picture on the right. The bridge is now usually known as Kingsmills Bridge. The brewery which gave it its original name stood on the open ground in front of the cathedral

The relationship with Locke was an important one for Johnstons. It lasted for fifty years and was often stormy for Locke was an autocratic character but it ended sadly in 1892 with a cryptic note in the ledger in red ink 'Bad Debt' against the balance of £55:7:8. The mighty Locke joined the long line of bankrupts which by then had included Macdougalls of Inverness.

There were two recurring problems which faced the Johnstons during these years. The first was caused by the location of the mill in a bend of the River Lossie. The mill lade – the channel feeding the water wheel which powered the mill – runs across this bend which encloses the factory and buildings rather like a slack bowstring. This channel can be seen today. The fall of the river was not great and the lade re-entered the river at a point where the river narrows sharply. As a result in times of heavy rain when the river was in flood the water backed up the lade, so much so that the wheel would cease to turn which stopped all the work at the mill and, if the river rose further, the mill would become flooded with consequent damage to goods and machinery. This problem was

A photograph dating from early in the twentieth century showing the effect of flooding in the mill. One wonders how long it took for everything to dry

first mentioned in 1852 in a letter of credit to Hastings and Miller of Leeds which describes the press papers they supplied being wet through the first day they were used '…by a sudden swelling of the river during the night' – one imagines however that it must have occurred frequently before. There is another mention in a letter dated 9th January, 1867 written by his mill manager to James Johnston in London where he was on a sales trip:

> 'It has been a terrible night of wind and rain and the river has risen in consequence it is just over the blowpipe of the engine & still rising so that there is little prospect of anything being done today.'

The problem was not finally solved until the 1950s when a dam and sluice were constructed to control the level of water.

The other main problem which is a recurring theme particularly in James Johnston's correspondence is the difficulty experienced in getting suitable staff, particularly of managerial capacity. There is a table of people employed which shows a workforce of between thirty-eight and forty-three in the years 1838–42, of these there were

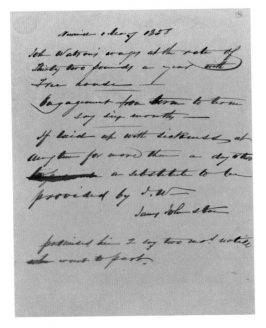

A note in James Johnston's handwriting dated 1st May, 1858. This served as the contract of employment for John Watson who would probably have been a weaver. The wages were thirty-two pounds a year with free house. The agreement ran for six months at a time and he was promised two months notice as James cryptically put it '...when want to part'

two designated as Foreman and assistant and between eleven and fifteen weavers. Very often, when they required a skilled workman, they had to look to the South, generally the Borders or Yorkshire and in many cases they would ask their suppliers whether they knew anyone suitable. In a letter to his card clothing supplier in Leeds James asked whether they knew of a competent hand who could take charge of:

> '...the engines and teazing alone – Do you know of anyone you think would suit me and I shall be much obliged if you can recommend me a good hand at a moderate wage say 20/–.'

Mill managers were a particular problem although it is difficult to tell whether James's judgement was faulty or whether he was just hard to please, probably a bit of both.

On 5th April, 1848 he advertised for a Mill Manager & Foreman at Newmill, Elgin in the *North British Advertiser* and got ten replies. He engaged John Ramage who was from Paisley. Ramage doesn't seem to have lasted long because in 1850 James was advertising again. This time he got thirteen applications. How and where he interviewed the applicants is not recorded but the jotter in which he made notes of many things about the mill and his staff records comments such as '...wants practice', '...has too much to say' against various of the applicants. He appointed a man from Galashiels but three months later he was writing to another supplier Messrs Ramsden, Harrison & Co of Halifax:

> 'I am not at all satisfied with my present Mill Manager a Galashiels man whom I got only 3 mos ago – can you recommend me a very good carder to take his place? The wages I allow are £60(£2170) a year, with free house garden and Gas, & his duties to look after the Teazing, Carding, Slubbing and Spinning of 2 sets of machines, one on coarse, the other on fine wools, he must of course besides knowing his business be an active steady & respectable man.
>
> If you know any such you think likely to suit, please let me know at once, & if not I shall be obliged by your making some inquiries for me. Meantime I am Gent^m Yours respectfully.'

In 1853 he was back in the market again.

The Story of
Johnstons of Elgin

Consolidation & Expansion
1850 – 1900

By the middle of the nineteenth century the firm had been in existence over fifty years. One wonders whether there were any celebrations when that landmark was passed but somehow reading of the hours worked, 6am to 6pm in summer and 7am to 7pm in the winter months, one doubts whether time would have been allowed. In 1850 we even find James writing to the Factory Inspector asking whether he was allowed to make up '...for the reduced work of Saturday'. It must be remembered that such hours were normal in factories then and were governed by legislation.

The company was certainly well established by 1850 and the next twenty years saw considerable changes most of which reflected the energies and various interests of James Johnston. Some of these were good and some bad. There was a disastrous foray into the export market in Australia in 1853 which showed James at his most impetuous. Hearing of the gold rush he conceived the idea that there would be great demand for plaids and stout shooting suits.

Accordingly he wrote in February, 1853 to John Masson in London saying he would be sending out:

> '...a consignment of Men's Plaids and perhaps a few blankets to the "Diggins", where I think such things would sell well during the cold season. But having no correspondent in the Colony I take the liberty of requesting your advice and recommendation of a good party either in Sydney or Melbourne in whose hands to place them.'

The enterprise was pursued with vigour and determination. James organised all the local tailors to make the suits, the first shipment of a hundred and sixty plaids was sent to each of two contacts, and this was followed by thirty-six suits sent to Sydney on 24th February,

James Johnston from an undated photograph Chairman and Managing Director of Johnstons of Elgin , 1845–c1880

0263749

27178903

9005252903

A respectful request from the work force to be allowed to work from 6am to 6pm during the winter

Newmill 14th September 1863

James Johnston Esqe

Sir,

We the undersigned would feel ourselves laid under the deepest obligations, and would look upon it as a special act of kindness, if instead of what has hitherto been the custom of changing the hours; from 6 to 7 in the morning, you would be pleased to allow us to retain the present hours viz; from 6 to 6.

This we have no hesitation in saying would prevent the irregularity of attendance at the proper hour on Saturdays mornings; besides, while it would ensure an equal amount of work performed, would be of incalculable benefit to us; as a Winter evening to a working man is a matter of great value.

William Russell
Robert Orr   Aby Davidson
John Mackie   Angus Campbell
Wm Moxon   William Brown
James Scott   John Smith
Alexander Welsh   James Shaw
Alexander Sutter   James Brown
George Davidson   John Fraser
James Williamson   Charles Moxon
Adam Legg   William Douglas
Thomas Dawson   Hugh McDonald
John Barclay
Andrew Clerk
James Black
Mark Reavely
George Thompson
Charles Fraser
Donald Cameron
John McPherson
James Sutter
Angus Fraser

1853 and a similar lot to Melbourne ten days later. By the end of March two hundred and ninety-nine jackets, two hundred and fifty-nine vests and two hundred and forty-one pairs of trousers were ready for shipment and by the middle of April he had made five shipments to Sydney and three to Melbourne. In the summer he was writing again to Masson telling him that:

> 'Early in July I shall have a case of apparel for each port made from my thinnest stuffs.'

It appears at first that the reaction from the agents in Australia was favourable but James had charged ahead without careful enough thought and Nemesis was waiting in the wings. There were the inevitable delays in communication but by 1856 news finally reached him that the shipments had been badly eaten by the moth and the suits had failed to sell as their cut was considered old-fashioned. In a letter to Gill Fowler & Co, Melbourne of 11th September, 1856 acknowledging receipt of their bill for £112:19:8 (£3716) James stated:

> '…the moth-eating may account for the £120 deficiency but the return of the clothing part (£68 nett here) is little more than half what I paid the tailors for making and furnishings, and considerably less than nothing for the cloth furnished myself.'

Only a brave man would have considered an enterprise of this type and the heading of the original entry in the Ledger *Speculation to Sydney* perhaps indicates that James was well aware of the risks.

A copy of a letter from Robert Gill who ran a weaving mill at Innerleithen just south of Peebles promising cashmere. He became a great friend of James Johnston and wrote amusingly to him about trade and the political situation around the world

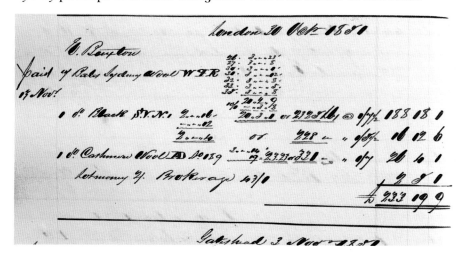

The first entry in the Day Book and Ledger for the purchase of cashmere in 1851. Cashmere was not used as much as vicuna in the nineteenth century but has since become the most important fibre used by Johnstons

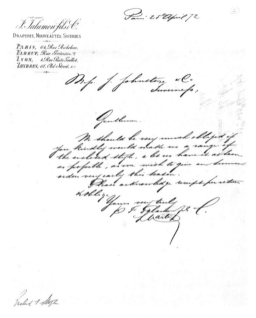

A request from F Talamon fils & Co of Paris for a range of patterns. Export orders boomed through the nineteenth century as Johnstons exploited the European markets

The very insignificant diploma awarded after the Paris Exhibition of 1867

On the other hand there was increasing use of vicuna during the period although the amount purchased varied enormously from year to year. From the ledgers it would seem that much of the vicuna was used for plaids and shawls and Macdougalls of Inverness was a ready customer, first for plaids and then for cloth which was cut into scarves. On 30th October, 1851 Newmill purchased their first ever lot of cashmere from E Buxton of Basinghall Street, London and it is of interest that on the same invoice one of the items was for 2725lbs of Sydney wool. The finer wool from the Merino sheep of Australia was already eating into the demand for the Cheviot wool from the Highlands.

James was always prepared to experiment with different fibres for as well as cashmere he also tried llama – he purchased eighty-four pounds on 31st January, 1851 – and in 1857 he experimented with something called vegetable wool which had been supplied by Buxtons as a sample. James was obviously charmed by the wool which he called a '...soft, silky and pretty substance' but in practice it didn't work and in the same letter he wrote:

'I think I may be able to make more of the silk waste and I should like you to get me 40 or 50lbs of it to experiment upon.'

There is no record of anything coming of this suggestion.

In the 1860s James moved on and tried camel hair – he bought two hundred and nine pounds in March, 1861 – mohair, Shetland wool and increasing quantities of cashmere and vicuna. During the 1860s the amount of vicuna purchased rose from 2600lbs in 1860 to a peak of 5400lbs in 1865 which produced a corresponding increase in turnover to £16,690(£635,555) in that year. The increase in the use of vicuna is quite startling considering that in 1857 only 78lbs was purchased but this must have been influenced by the price of the material which had dropped dramatically from 7s:6d per pound in 1857 to only 3s per pound in 1865.

It was during this period that Johnstons started to exhibit at international exhibitions. James took part in the National Exhibition in London in 1851 and the Paris Exhibition of 1855. There is a record of the mauds and cloths that he exhibited in London and the collection covered every quality of cloth that Johnstons produced except llama. Interestingly one of the entries was for *One*

Inverleithen
19 Aug.t 1863

My dear Sir

I send you Dawn's patterns 2 sendings together, the one followed the other before I got you the first despatched, being rather busted and taken up with one thing and another—

Have you got any more work in? we have as yet only a little but have a great deal more offering if it would only come, from Foreign Houses to whom we have made and are making no end of t.yds for their travellers which is a great nuisance to begin with—

Every mill in this countryside is full of work, running every one of them overtime— many all the night through— besides getting work done in Yorkshire, Alloa and elsewhere— I am provoked to think we should not share in this, and that my activity is failing I wish we had our Railway made but! that 12 miles of road is as much a barrier to buyers who flock to Galashiels as if we were located beyond the Rocky mountains I get bits of orders dropping in from the East Indies as frequently as from Glasgow or London, what do you think of you and me going over them with our wally Bags and swatches, when the new air carriages that are coming out will fly us over in about a week I do not hear yet that refreshment rooms are being built in the clouds on the route, but no doubt these will form part of the enterprise as sandwiches must become too stale even for so short a journey

I trust Mrs Johnstone and you are enjoying the vacation time with your scholars at home beside you, this is some compensation I find for the disappointments we get in business—

With very kind regards to you all
Yours very truly
Robert Gill

James Johnstone Esq

Maud of Dyed Australian Wool in imitation of Vicuna. He exhibited again in London and Paris in 1862 and 1867 respectively and at the Paris exhibition he was awarded a diploma.

About this time James started to expand his export markets and the 1860s saw the start of sales to Italy and France and these were followed in the next ten years by increased sales to Germany and Belgium and further afield to South America and Japan. France was the main market on the continent, by 1880 there were over twenty customers, mainly in Paris, and James may well have had an agent

One of Robert Gill's best letters bemoaning the lack of the railway from Galashiels to Innerleithen and foretelling both air travel, hot air balloons were the rage at the time, and the type of meals that were to be available in the sky!

The 1865 building, now a Grade II listed building, which houses the shop and visitors centre. The original entry to the building was at the back and the 'reading room' was on the ground floor on the right

working in Paris who was responsible for this increase. It was not until 1882 that a start was made selling to the USA which for many years was the main export market for the firm.

The expansion of the company in the middle of the nineteenth century was dramatic. In the 1850s the lowest turnover in that decade was £4,840 (£162,866) (1854) and the highest, £10,970 (£417,737) (1859), in the 1860s the comparable figures were £8,260 (£298,764) (1861) and £16,690 (£635,555) (1865), and in the 1870s they were £17,150 (£620,315) (1870) and £35,910 (£1,298,864) (1875). This expansion was echoed by the building work that took place during those years the results of which can still be seen by everyone who visits Newmill today.

The main additions were the buildings erected in 1860s. The first of these is the building which now contains the shop. This was designed in 1865 and replaced a former building which was demolished to make way for it. The foundations of this older building can still be seen under the grass oval in front of the mill. James wrote to his lawyer Alexander Cameron of Elgin about the insurance of the new building on 10th August, 1865:

> 'Policy for a new detached Building, 3 stories high and 100 feet long running at right angles to the dwelling house marked No.6 on the sketch. It is not yet quite finished inside but it is intended for:– on the ground floor a Reading Room for Work people, a Sales Room and office. On 2nd floor one room for Wool and another for Goods, and on the 3rd floor a wool store. I annex the values I wish insured and requesting your attention am Yours truly.'

The total value for insurance was £5900 (£22,467) of which the building was only £800. In 1867 there were more dramatic developments as the main two-storey building which had been put up in

The Aimers Maclean plan for the 1868 building greatly reduced in size. The position of the new pillars has been marked in at a later date

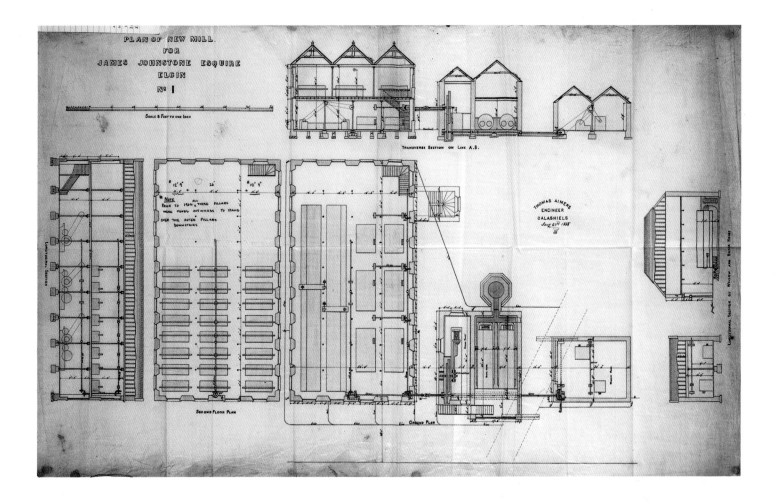

1860 to house the looms was burned down. James wrote to Messrs H. Cooper & Co, a yarn customer in Aberdeen, two days after the fire:

'I regret to say a serious fire took place here on Sunday morning completely destroying the building in which I had my Warping Twisting & Finishing Machinery together with my Yarn store in which was nearly £3000 worth of yarn but partially insured.'

Receipt for the 1857 fire insurance certificate

James wrote at once to Platt Brothers of Oldham, his machinery suppliers, for advice on rebuilding and on their advice Aimers Maclean, a textile engineering firm of Galashiels, were retained. Three buildings were erected of which the two largest, the boiler house and the weaving and spinning shed, remain substantially unaltered although their use has changed. The plans for these buildings have survived.

In 1871 two further buildings were put up, the largest was a Yarnstore, Pattern Weaving, Hand Warping and Winding Shop which cost £550 (£19,893) and the smaller one was the start of the present dye house and cost £210 (£7595). Charles Johnston wrote to his insurers asking the rate for '…a new Dye house we have just put up: stone and slated, three furnaces fired from the outside.'

It is difficult to be precise about the machinery that was purchased during the early years of the firm. No list was ever compiled on an annual basis, and it was not until 1870 that James made a complete list for valuation purposes. This showed under the various production elements; yarn production: three carding setts (one

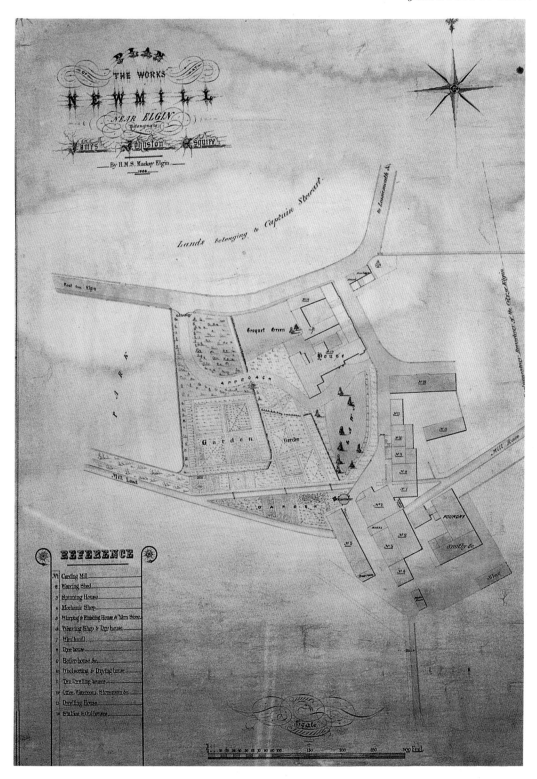

The map of Newmill drawn for James Johnston in 1866. The original hangs in the board room

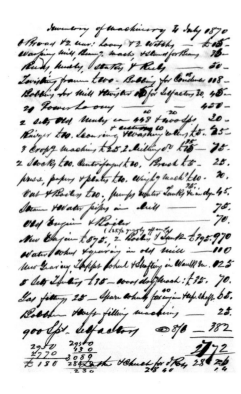

The list of machinery compiled by James Johnston in 1870. Unlike most of his contemporaries his handwriting is difficult to decipher and the boldness of his script seems to reflect his character

fine and two Cheviot), two pairs of mules; weaving: one warp mill, six broad and two narrow handlooms, twenty-one power looms; finishing: two milling machines, two pairs of stocks, one raiser, three croppers, one brush, one hydraulic press and five sets of tenters.

Tenters were spiked frames on which the cloth was hooked and stretched out for drying. This took place in the open air although it is not clear whether it was done Dutch-barn fashion under a roof or not. Although this method of drying was ideal for the cloth that was made, in certain weather conditions nothing dried at all. A note from Alexander Johnston in 1837 to Urquhart, Blackwood & Co, a merchant in Glasgow states:

'The weather, however, has been such for the last ten days as stopped all drying and enables me only to send you as annexed which hope may meet approval.'

A tentering machine, a Whitely steam dryer, was ordered and finally installed in 1875 and another list of machinery, made in 1873, records not only that an extra carding sett had been installed but that there were thirty-three power looms compared with twenty three years earlier.

In 1880 James Johnston was sixty-five. History does not relate whether he retired then or not but it seems possible for within five years the fortunes of the firm started to decline. The turnover reached a peak in 1882 when it touched £34,920 (£1,365,721) but by 1892 it was down to £14,720 (£665,638) and the amount of wool used also declined sharply. Whether James retired or not the fortunes of the firm would have declined anyway during this period.

The great foreign trade boom collapsed in 1873 and the period from then until the 1890s is often known as 'The Great Depression'. Europe started introducing protectionist tariffs in the 1870s and, while these tariffs made little difference to start with, the introduction of the McKinley tariff in America in 1890 had a marked impact. This tariff followed by the Dingley legislation of 1897 doubled the price of Scottish woollen goods in the American market and decimated trade with the USA. Johnstons was not immune from this effect.

It must be said that there were other causes of the general decline in the woollen trade in the last twenty years of the nineteenth century; overcapacity, brought about by improved technology was one; increased competition from Europe was another and a general loss of confidence on the part of the manufacturers themselves. As at Johnstons many firms were now in their third generation and in some cases the energy and drive of the founders of the industry no longer existed. Charles Johnston did not fall into this category. By the turn of the century the activities of the firm had stabilised, turnover had risen to just under £25,960 (£1,252,050) and the amount of wool used had also increased. In the export field the USA started to order and the famous Brooks Brothers store in New York placed their first order in 1893. The Platt looms which had been used for many years were replaced by Hutchinson Hollingworth Dobcross looms twenty of which were bought before 1900 and more floor space was added to the factory. It was also in this period that Ernest Johnston appeared in the firm's books for the first time. He worked mainly in London on the sales side and he is first mentioned in the Journal on 31st July, 1891.

Johnstons thus profited from the new technology and were able to enter the twentieth century with confidence.

Customers for over a hundred years. The famous Brooks Brothers label of New York woven in Newmill in 1994 for today's orders for quality cashmere goods

Charles Johnston. Chairman and Managing Director of Johnstons of Elgin, c1885–1920
From a scratched old photograph

The final extension to the weaving shed built in 1911 with the huge brick chimney. The 1868 two-storey building shows in the rear and the two gables with the round windows are the end of the dye house. The small building in between housed the gas engine which powered the looms. The wall of the weaving extension was built of brick so there may have been some thought of extending the building further

One of the big gas engine flywheels being installed in 1908. Charles Johnston is on the extreme left. The holes on the face of the wheel were for a crowbar to get the wheel turning for starting

The Story of
Johnstons of Elgin

The Twentieth Century

By the end of the nineteenth century Alexander, James and Charles Johnston, grandfather to grandson, had run Johnstons for over a hundred years. In the twentieth century the same pattern was repeated but in 1920 the ownership changed and the family who ran the company for the next seventy years became the Harrisons.

In September 1904 Edward Harrison joined Johnstons as assistant to Ernest Johnston, Charles Johnston's son. Ernest was in charge of the sales office in London and Edward was to help him in that role. Soon after this Andrew Boyd (AB as he became known) also joined the company and he went to assist Ernest in the sales office while Edward Harrison stayed in Elgin and concentrated on production. These appointments might have had little effect on the succession but Ernest Johnston was killed in the War and, with no son to succeed him, Charles Johnston sold his interest in the firm to Edward Harrison and Andrew Boyd who became the junior partner.

Edward Harrison came from a well-known family of Edinburgh woollen merchants. For the next forty-six years until 1966 when he finally retired at the age of eighty-eight he was the guiding force behind the fortunes of Johnstons. He was a remarkable man. His main interests lay in the design and production of cloth. He was a keen amateur photographer and an accomplished painter who exhibited at the RSA. Donald Williams, who started working for Johnstons when he was fourteen in 1922, recalls that he was usually to be found in the design studio. John Harrison, his nephew, who started working in the firm in 1955 describes his dynamism:

> 'He was keenly interested in everything. He was one of those people who was always ready to experiment and it was this willingness which helped the firm in the 1920s at the height of the depression.'

Edward Harrison, 1878–1977.
Chairman and Managing Director of
Johnstons of Elgin, 1920–66

Scenes from Johnstons' factory in the early 1900s

Top: The installation of the Lancashire boiler which heated and powered the mill in the early part of the twentieth century

Below: The finishing department

The great wedding picnic at Gordon Castle to celebrate Edward Harrison's wedding Saturday, June 26th 1908

Ned Harrison recalls how his father was a member of a delegation sent to America by the Scottish Woollen Manufacturers Association. While he was there he realised that there was a demand for cloths lighter and looser than those normally supplied by the Scottish woollen mills and on his return he started to experiment with the production of lightweight cloth. Johnstons gradually evolved a range of cloth suitable for the American market. It was a significant trip for on it Edward met Mr Magnus of Magnus Imports. This meeting started the trade in scarves with America which has continued to this day and it was largely through these initiatives that Johnstons survived the years of recession in the 1920s and 1930s.

The Harrisons continued the Johnstons' tradition of re-investing the profits in the business and the years between the wars saw a significant increase in the buildings and new machinery. The first new building of the twentieth century took place in 1911 when a further extension was added to the original post-fire building of 1868 which made space for more looms and effectively brought this building to its present size. There was another major building event in the same year when five bays were added to the original mill building. This extension was first planned as a home for the cloth raising machines and it later became the pattern weaving

area before that was moved to the main weaving shed. In 1993 it became the sales administration centre and will probably change yet again back to finishing.

At the end of the 1920s a building had been planned on the west side of the site at Newmill as a home for the carding and spinning machinery. The building was to be on slightly higher ground and would be immune from the floods which were not finally conquered until 1951. In spite of the Depression and the dismal outlook for trade in general the decision was taken to carry on with this building and it was completed in 1930. The carding and spinning machinery was moved into it in the same year. The materials and paintwork were superb and have survived untouched for over sixty years. This was a signal act of faith in the future of Johnstons.

The company also made significant changes to the power supply at the mill. When the new buildings were erected in the 1860s and early 1870s the power for the factory was supplied by a central

The entrance to the mill as it looks today. The buildings put up in the early years of the 20th century are behind the tower

Ned Harrison, born 1918
Chairman and Managing Director of
Johnstons of Elgin, 1966–78
From a photograph taken early in 1940

steam engine assisted by the waterwheel. This was a rather cumbersome arrangement and meant that if anything went wrong with the engine the whole factory came to a standstill. In 1908 four separate gas-driven engines each with large heavy flywheels were installed at strategic points throughout the plant to serve each of the departments. The gas to drive the engines was generated on the premises and at the end of 1908 on 26th December of that year the waterwheel and 'Auld Scotland' as the 1868 steam engine was known stopped for the last time. The bed stones of Auld Scotland were used to form an arched entrance to the building opposite the boiler house. This power supply lasted until 1930 when two large steam turbines were installed in the old part of the mill opposite the boiler house. These turbines drove generators which powered electric motors and these supplied power individually to all the departments. This arrangement lasted until 1938 when the company switched over to the national grid although nowadays back-up generators are available to cope with power cuts.

In 1936 Ned Harrison came into the firm when he left school at eighteen to start a five year apprenticeship. His career with Johnstons was interrupted by the war but he returned in 1945 and became a Director in 1954. Ned Harrison succeeded his father when he retired in 1966 and he retired himself in 1978 when he was sixty. Unlike his father he had no ambition to work until his eighties. He was succeeded by his cousin, another Harrison, John who had joined the company in 1955. John became a Director in 1963 and succeeded Ned as Chairman in 1978 an office that he still holds in a non-executive capacity. To complete the picture James Sugden who had joined Johnstons in 1986 as Sales Director became Managing Director in 1987. Johnstons is now therefore run by a Yorkshire spinning man but as it approaches the twenty-first century there is no lessening in the confidence within the firm while the pace of expansion has increased.

It is harder to convey the impression of Johnstons in the early twentieth century than the nineteenth. The records are not so full and the correspondence books which give such insights into the trading methods of James Johnston do not exist. However talking to people who worked for the company during the 1920s and '30s reveals a period of calm certainty when nothing appeared to change

One of Edward Harrison's crayon drawings looking south from The Bield, the Harrison's family home, towards Rothes. The hill in the distance is Brown Muir. He exhibited at the RSA and a number of his pictures are hung in the entrance hall of the office

very much. One foreman who was away for five years during the war was told on his return to '…go and get the oil-can, it's in the same place.' Ned Harrison himself remarked how little anything had altered '…It was just like coming home to something familiar' – which indeed it was.

The turnover figures available confirm this impression. The turnover at the turn of the century was £25,960 (£1,211,812) and this increased to a peak of £134,430 (£2,161,634) in 1920. The turnover then declined throughout the 1920s and '30s and in 1932 was only £39,970 (£1,112,365). Thereafter it started to rise again.

However the Second World War had its effect. At the beginning all the Territorial members of staff were called up at once. Key personnel were exempt from conscription but there were great shortages of male workers and the conditions within the mill altered greatly. Wool supplies were rationed, all woollen companies had to make a quota of khaki cloth and 'utility' cloths for sale on coupons and after those two requirements had been met cloth could be made for export to the USA and the West.

It seems strange to think that export trade continued throughout the war in spite of the threat from submarines but it was a vital part of the war effort and encouraged by the Government to earn valuable dollars. In particular scarves continued to be sent to

Above: Leaving work in the 1950s. The 1865 building is in the background

Below: John Harrison, born 1932 Chairman of Johnstons of Elgin Managing Director 1978–87

America throughout the war by parcel post. The American business was conducted by Mr Magnus of Magnus Imports but he died during the war and his widow asked Johnstons and Pringles of Hawick whose lines he agented whether they would buy the business. Johnstons did not have the money available at that time but Pringle bought the business which was re-named Pringle Johnston. It continues to this day as Pringle of Scotland.

When the war ended in 1945 demand for all goods outstripped supply. There was no question of having to sell any product. Everything that could be made had an automatic market and the main customers of the firm had to be rationed. Buyers, no doubt hoping for preferential treatment, started visiting Newmill instead of waiting in their headquarters in London or the Borders for Andrew Boyd to call. This situation applied in reverse to Newmill's own suppliers. New machinery was virtually unobtainable. A new carding machine had to be ordered one and a half to two years in advance and for several years the company struggled to meet pro-

Two photographs of the 1957 fire. In a sense Johnstons were lucky as there was little material held in the buildings which were burnt

duction targets. There was no time to think of new products and there was no necessity to look for new markets or seek expansion. This situation started to change around 1960 when it became easier to get new machines.

During this period the firm showed steady if unspectacular expansion. Ignoring the fluctuations of the war years the turnover increased throughout the 1950s and '60s from £181,050(£3,119,491) in 1950 to £716,110 (£5,599,980) in 1970.

In 1966 Edward Harrison finally retired to be replaced by his son Ned. Ned Harrison claims that he was only a titular head of the company and spent much of his time involved in local government. In this he was following a long tradition of involvement in local affairs by the head of Johnstons. James Johnston had been Provost

Among the many notable people to visit Johnstons over the years have been the two 'first' Prime Ministers of this century. Ramsay Macdonald, the first Labour Prime Minister visited Johnstons in 1933. He is seen with Edward Harrison

Margaret Thatcher, first woman Prime Minister visited Johnstons in 1982 during the General Election campaign of that year. John Harrison is behind her

of Elgin in the nineteenth century and Edward Harrison also. But he is being over-modest for it was when he took over that the first significant steps were taken which altered the structure of the company and started its current expansion and prosperity. These were the takeovers in 1966 and 1967 of Bradleys and Reid and Welsh respectively. W J Bradley was an important London scarf wholesaler and Reid and Welsh was the scarf division of another Elgin manufacturer. The initial impact of these takeovers was traumatic for the year following the takeover of Bradleys many of the scarf wholesalers in Britain placed no orders with Johnstons. In the long run however the takeovers helped to set in place the vertical integration of the company and as the influence of the wholesalers fell away production bottlenecks eased. The philosophy of make big sell small with the additional profit margins that this process creates is one of the guiding stars of the firm's success.

The years after the war also saw the final solution to the old problem of flooding when a dam was built in 1951 at the tail of the mill race to prevent the river backing up. I suspect that the directors wondered why the solution to this problem had taken so long.

In 1957 there was another large fire which burnt out the old part of the mill. Luckily there was little equipment in the building at the time of the fire and actual damage was slight. The building was replaced immediately. Two further buildings were added in the 1950s. They replaced the old teazing house and this brought all the yarn supplies under one roof.

The company expanded rapidly during this period and the turnover increased from £493,020 (£5,058,385) in 1964 to £3,374,580 (£8,605,179) in 1979. In 1978 Ned Harrison retired as he had promised at the age of sixty and he was succeeded by his cousin, John Harrison.

John had started work at Elgin in 1955 when he left Cambridge University. He describes Edward Harrison as a remarkable, dynamic man whose judgement he respected but he admits that during the immediate post-war years Johnstons failed to establish themselves in the burgeoning market in Europe and continued to rely on trade with America. At the end of the 1950s American trade was torpedoed by tariffs introduced by Eisenhower which were similar in size and effect to the McKinley tariffs of the 1890s. This forced the company to look for new markets in Europe and the Far East and after some delay Johnstons returned to both markets with considerable and continuing success..

At the same time the company started to re-equip their production facilities. Because their production rate was low the old spinning mules were scrapped and ring spinning frames installed. However, as the demand for finer and finer cloths increased, these frames were not found to be really suitable for the production of the fine yarns that were needed even after considerable adaptation and they were also unsuitable for the yarn required by the Hawick hosiery plant. So some computer-controlled mule spinning was reintroduced and the ring frames further upgraded. The carding machines were added to and replaced where necessary and to improve the quality of the yarn the old, rather crude, wool drying system was replaced by a modern RF dryer (in effect a glorified microwave oven) at the cost of over £300,000.

Most of the old Dobcross looms were replaced by Dornier rapier looms which were both faster and kinder to the yarn. These Dorniers are being continually updated and the ones in place now

Yarn strings in the design studio at Johnstons of Elgin. The considerable growth of Johnstons at the end of the twentieth century has meant a huge expansion in the design capacity of the company and a large investment in designers and new design premises. These are being constructed as this book goes to press and when complete will occupy one of the three floors of the completely refurbished 1860s building. Yarn strings, the fundamental tools of all textile designers will occupy pride of place in the new studios

A view of the Hawick knitting factory showing the large investment in the finest modern plant

weave at twice the speed of the first models. Some of the old Dobcross looms have been retained and they are used for pattern weaving, a task which is less suited to the high-performance Dorniers. To complete the yarn improvements a state-of-the-art yarn package dyeing and drying installation was put in at the cost of £250,000 and similar improvements were made to cloth finishing. The process of re-equipment is a continuing one.

At the end of the 1960s the company ignored precedent and invested in knitwear. The object was to take full advantage of its considerable skills and experience in cashmere. However this venture foundered because of the discovery of oil in the North Sea and the oil boom that swept through the north of Scotland at that time. It is true to say that nearly every available man in that part of the

world left to work on the oil rigs to the extent as John Harrison noted that it was impossible to get your car serviced at a garage. The knitwear enterprise therefore foundered on the lack of skilled labour but five years later the opportunity arose to lease the old Blenkhorn Richardson building in Hawick from the Scottish Development Agency and a knitwear operation was started up.

This has gone from strength to strength. The building has been purchased and expanded and today Johnstons has one of the most sophisticated weaving and knitting plants in the world. The company has expanded dramatically in the last part of the twentieth century, the turnover has risen from £716,110 in 1970 to nearly £27,000,000 in 1994 and in 1993–4 a further thirty thousand square feet was added to the buildings. The whole company operates on the principle that only the best is good enough and this philosophy extends from purchasing – the company buys the finest raw materials – through design to manufacture and completion.

In both 1978 and 1994 Johnstons was awarded the Queen's Award for Export and the company is renowned throughout the world for the excellence of its products.

The party held to celebrate the Queen's Award in 1994 was possibly less formal than the wedding picnic illustrated on page 68

Left: James Sugden, Managing Director of Johnstons of Elgin since 1987 in the kilt with (from the left) Robert Harrison, John Harrison's son and Messrs Mozumi, Ogushi and Nakai, one of Johnstons' distributors from Tokyo

Right: Waiting for lunch (from the right) Air Vice Marshal, George Chesworth, CB, OBE, DFC, Her Majesty's Lord Lieutenant for Morayshire who presented the award on behalf of The Queen, next to him is Mrs Chesworth, and then come a family group of Jenny Urquhart, Ned Harrison's granddaughter, Heather Urquhart, Ned Harrison's daughter and Linda Harrison, Robert Harrison's wife

A cashmere goat

The Cashmere Story

Cashmere must be one of the most evocative words in the world. It conjures up images of soft luxury and warmth, and calls to mind the high mountains of the Himalayas.

What is cashmere and where does it come from? As its name implies cashmere originated in Kashmir. It is the fibre spun from the inner fleece of the cashmere goat and is one of the finest fibres known to man. Cashmere is produced in Mongolia, China, Iran and Afghanistan. The finest cashmere comes from Inner Mongolia where the fibre has a thickness of between 14.5 and 16.5 microns with a micron measuring 0.00004 of an inch. Iranian cashmere is slightly coarser and measures between 17.5 and 18.5 microns.

The goats which produce this luxury fibre are part of the nomadic life of the tribesmen of the Himalayas. Sometime towards the end of the eighteenth century the main tribes migrated north-

Herding cashmere goats in Inner Mongolia

Photographs taken by Donald Montgomery, Johnstons' production director on a trip to Inner Mongolia with James Sugden to buy cashmere

Above the goatherd with his goats and on the right combing out the fibre

east from Kashmir in the North of India and finally settled in Inner Mongolia. There they stayed and Mongolia came to be the main cashmere producing area in the world. It is hard to understand how the luxury of cashmere can be associated with the barren life of the Himalayan foothills, where the weather is dry and arid in the summer months and many degrees below freezing in the winter. But it is these conditions which create the right climate for the goats to grow their two coats, the outer coat which is hard and wiry and the inner fibre which is so soft and luxurious. In the spring the goats start to moult and it is then that the fibre is combed away by hand, each animal producing about four ounces of hair. Combing the goats and collecting the fibre is a family occasion similar to the *vendange* in France, hard, back-breaking work worlds away from the fashion houses of the textile industries in Scotland and Italy.

After the fibre has been combed out it is collected and baled and then transported down to the trading ports formerly on mules, nowadays with roads being built throughout China, partly by mule and partly by lorry. Cashmere comes in three colours, grey brown and white. Pure white is the most prized for it can be dyed the palest colours and it commands the highest price.

The transformation of the fibre into cloth is a difficult process and contributes to the mystique of cashmere. It is complicated because the inner and outer coats of the goats are mixed in together and have to be separated, 'de-haired', before the fine fibre can be spun and woven.

In the nineteenth century this was done by hand but towards the end of that century Dawsons and Johnstons separately developed a process which separated the fibres by machine. For many years mechanical de-hairing was a closely kept industrial secret but nowadays de-hairing by machine is relatively commonplace and most cashmere today is bought de-haired from China who have developed their own de-hairing industry in the last twenty years using Japanese technology.

Cashmere has been known and prized for centuries. Cashmere shawls found their way to the courts of the Roman Emperors. In the fifteenth century thousands of workers were employed in the city of Srinagar weaving carpets and shawls. Cashmere shawls from Srinagar were popularised in Europe by Empress Eugenie, wife of Napoleon III and a leader of world fashion in the nineteenth century. There is a portrait of her wearing one and she is generally given the credit for introducing cashmere to the western world.

It is also intimately associated with Scotland and this connection is one of those happy accidents which comes together from a number of strands. The Scots were always traders and explorers. They travelled to the Far East and established those trading companies which today have world-wide reputations. The Scots also had a large indigenous weaving industry and they also had the need for warm clothing in the winter.

History relates that in the early 1850s a Scot travelling from the Far East returned home to Elgin with a bale of raw cashmere which

Left: Sorting cashmere fibre by hand before de-hairing

Right: Willowing cashmere in Xing Jiang, China to get rid of the dust

Cashmere from Mongolia is purchased through the official Chinese Government bodies. This letter notified Johnstons of a sub-division in the appropriate corporation

he sold to James Johnston. This was the first time that Johnstons of Elgin had dealt with cashmere and was the forerunner of the present prosperity of the company.

There is a twist to this story in that the fibre was far more likely to have been vicuna from South America which was first recorded as being used by Johnstons in 1849. On the 30th October, 1851 there is an entry in the ledger for the purchase of cashmere from the wool merchants Buxtons of Basinghall Street, London and James bought another small lot in 1853 but the main luxury fibre used by Johnstons for most of the nineteenth century was vicuna.

Vicunas are extremely difficult to domesticate and during the nineteenth century the animals were indiscriminately slaughtered to secure their pelts. By the middle of the twentieth century they were on the verge of extinction and this slaughter was banned. In 1973 it became illegal to import vicuna without an official licence from South America and the supply dried up completely.

Whether the intransigence of the vicuna resulted in the emergence of cashmere as the luxury fibre must remain an arguable point. What is certain is that cashmere now is synonymous with all that is finest in woven goods and is a benchmark for the best Scottish tweeds and knitwear.

Johnstons' involvement with cashmere started in the middle of

Combing cashmere goats in Scotland

the nineteenth century and has continued to this day. Johnstons has always maintained direct links with China, buying first from the China merchants and nowadays buying direct from the Chinese Commodities Export Committee. James Sugden, the Managing Director visits China twice a year, attends the Trade Fairs at Canton by invitation, a great honour, and has recently set up a joint Johnstons – China company to ensure a continuing supply of de-haired cashmere for Johnstons. In world terms while Johnstons still rank some way behind Dawsons, the leading spinners of cashmere, they account for up to five per cent of the world crop annually and their demand for cashmere is gradually increasing.

Supply has never been constant. During the Korean War it dried up completely but in the last twenty years the market has been stabilised and the producers have been grouped together under the banner of the Central Committee. At the same time the Chinese have made great steps in improving the husbandry of the goats and a breeding programme has been introduced to produce a better quality of fibre and a higher percentage of white fibre. The price set by the Central Committee varies from year to year and there have been attempts to create alternative sources of supply in Scotland and Australia, where Dawsons tried to set up an industry. Australian cashmere turned out to have more the properties of

Vicuna in South America

The finished article. A label is sewn onto a cashmere jumper knitted in Johnstons' Hawick factory

mohair but Scottish cashmere shows some promise and in 1994 Johnstons de-haired the whole of the Scottish clip which amounted to nearly one thousand kilos of fibre. In 1988 Johnstons had produced a limited edition of scarves from the first ever Scottish cashmere crop which at that date amounted to just fifty-four kilos. This could truly have been called the first Scottish cashmere product.

While Johnstons continued to use cashmere for over a hundred and fifty years as a main source of fibre for fine cloths, shawls and accessories, the knitting industry was developed at a later stage. Hawick has been the home of knitting establishments in Scotland for over a hundred years. Initially the industry used the local wools and was particularly successful in making up fully fashioned underwear in Pure New Wool. In the 1920s Scottish knitwear for jerseys and outwear became more fashionable and, along with the finest imported lambswools, cashmere was introduced as being the finest and softest fibre available for this growing market. The foundation of the Border knitwear industry was born, with classics such as the twin set, and the softest cashmere garments created with the skills of expert finishers. This and the soft local water with which Hawick is blessed laid the foundation for the blossoming cashmere knitwear industry. Johnstons entered this industry in 1973 and their factory in Hawick keeps them in the forefront of this development

Cashmere is the most exciting material to work with. It is difficult to get hold of, it is produced in a remote primitive area of the world. It is complicated to process the fibre and it is very expensive. All the difficulties of dealing with cashmere remain the same and have remained the same for over a hundred and fifty years but it produces a wonderful product which Johnstons is proud to have been associated with for so many years. May this association long continue and prosper.

A Pistacia chinensis *growing at Newmill next to the dye house. This native of China is a rare tree to be found in the north of Scotland and it is a tribute to the mild climate of Elgin that it flourishes. Charles Johnston planted a large number of trees in the grounds of Newmill early in the 1900s including some Coastal redwoods,* Sequoia sempervirens. *It is probable that this tree was planted then but another more romantic suggestion is that a seed dropped from a bale of cashmere in the nineteenth century and germinated*

Scottish Estate Tweeds

THE PLATES

Note

The plates are all in alphabetical order starting with Aberchalder
and ending with Wyvis except where an estate has two tweed designs.
Where this occurs priority has been given to placing these designs
together on one page and this has meant some
minor adjustment in a few cases

The majority of the tweeds are shown actual size. There are a
few exceptions where the size of the cloth sample provided
for photography did not permit this

Ned Harrison examining one of the old patterns books showing a number of the estate tweeds for which Johnstons were famous in the nineteenth century. From the top on the left hand page are: Lochmore or Dundonnell, Ing, Ballindalloch, Brook, Guisachan and Erchless. On the right are Mar, Prince of Wales, Russell (Glenurquhart style), Glen Moriston, Fannich, Coigach or Baillie. The Prince of Wales and Russell have not been included in this edition as they are not, strictly speaking, estate tweeds

ABERCHALDER

The estate lies on the south-west side of Loch Oich which is part of the Caledonian Canal. It is owned by Miss Jean Ellice. The Ellice family bought Aberchalder, which was part of the Glen Garry estates, in 1860. They brought to Aberchalder the original tweed which Miss Balfour, later Mrs Ellice, had designed when her family were tenants at Glenfeshie and the tweed was used on their new estate. The tweed is now no longer used on the hill but it remains the origin of all Scottish estate tweeds. Although they were not necessarily the original makers Johnstons first invoiced the tweed to Macdougalls of Inverness on 22nd June, 1846.

ALTNAHARRA

The estate of Altnaharra lies in the middle of Sutherland, twenty miles to the north of Lairg and is the property of Gray and Adams Ltd of Fraserburgh. The tweed was introduced by Mr Laurence Kimball when he owned the estate in 1930.
The estate passed to Mr Marcus Kimball MP, later Lord Kimball, and was bought from him by Gray and Adams in 1992. The tweed was created by Hunters of Brora and the colour has varied over the years being now rather browner than the original which had a greener cast. The result is that the brown weft overcheck now sinks more into the ground. The design is basically a Shepherd check with overcheck and was supplied by Campbells of Beauly.

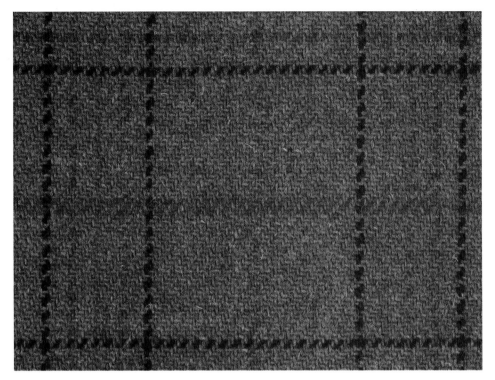

NORTH AFFRIC

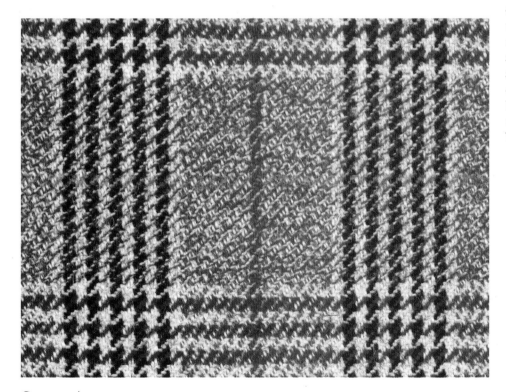

SOUTH AFFRIC

The estate lies in Glen Affric forty miles to the south-west of Inverness. Affric estate was originally owned by 'The Chisholm' but it was taken over by Highland Estates Ltd in the late 1920s to develop the water power. The estate was sold to Robert Wotherspoon, Lord Provost of Inverness, when Tom Johnston nationalised the power scheme. In 1950 Provost Wotherspoon sold the estate to the Forestry Commission but retained the lodge and sporting rights. Mr and Mrs Iain Wotherspoon took over the lodge and sporting rights in 1960 and bought back the northern part of the estate in 1983. Part of this was sold to Mr John Watson in 1990.

The estate is now in three parts, South Affric owned by the Forestry Commission, West Affric owned by the National Trust and North Affric owned by Mr John Watson.

There is some doubt about who designed the brown tweed which is used by the Wotherspoon family. It may have been Lord Furness who was a sporting tenant during the 1920s and '30s. The green tweed was adopted recently by Mr Wotherspoon as being more suitable for the hill and this pattern is now also used by Mr Watson and his stalkers.

The estate lies about nine miles south-west of Aberdeen and is owned by Lt-Colonel Robert A Campbell. His father, Lt-Colonel H A Campbell, OBE, DL, and Russells of Insch designed and introduced the tweed after Colonel Campbell bought the estate in 1952. The pattern is basically a Shepherd check but varied by using a different pair of colours for warp and weft resulting in a soft Lovat effect. Like many of the estate tweeds the colours have altered with changing manufacturers and the present version is somewhat lighter in depth than the original.

ALTRIES

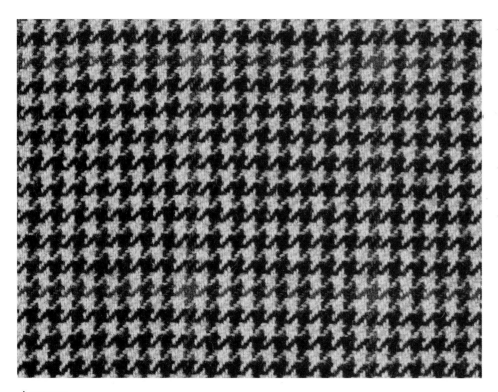

Altyre lies close to Forres in Moray and is owned by Sir William Gordon Cumming. The design was introduced about 1926 by Sir Alastair Gordon Cumming of Altyre and Gordonstoun. It is a slight variant of the basic Shepherd in that there is a little difference between the warp and weft light colour and it is overchecked in blue. It was made by Hunters of Brora and originally supplied through Campbells of Beauly. Altyre was one of the estates which features in the deer stalking classic, *Wild Sports of the Highlands* by Charles St John.

ALTYRE

The estate lies in the south-east corner of the Isle of Islay just off the west coast and belongs to Sir John MacTaggart, Bt and Sandy MacTaggart. The tweed was designed and produced by Haggarts of Aberfeldy and introduced to the estate by Jack MacTaggart about 1958. In the second half of the nineteenth century the estate was owned by the Ramsay family and was sold by them to the Clifton family early in the 1900s. The MacTaggarts acquired the estate in parcels between 1952–8.

ARDTALLA

Ardtalnaig is twelve miles west of Aberfeldy and is owned by a Moncrieffe Trust. Before that it belonged to a Berry Family Trust and the tweed illustrated is that one. Currently a new tweed is being designed by Miranda Moncrieffe which will be introduced at the end of 1994. Not obvious in the illustration is the quiet russet overchecking in the weft which is dominated by the warp check.

ARDTALNAIG

The estate lies about fifteen miles north-west of Oban on the Sound of Mull and is held in trust for members of the Raven family. They bought the estate from the late Gerard Craig Sellar in 1930. Before that it had been owned by the Smith family, ship's chandlers and distillers from London. The design is a simple brown and white Shepherd check. The shade has varied from time to time but the version illustrated is the original and first made in the Johnstons mills in 1905 and supplied to George Harrison of Edinburgh. In later versions the check is bigger.

ARDTORNISH

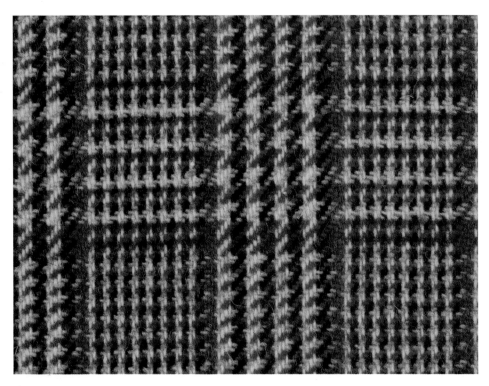

The estate lies about sixteen miles west of Newtonmore on the southern shores of Loch Laggan and is owned by the descendants of Sir John Ramsden who introduced the tweed about 1920. It was first made by Haggarts of Aberfeldy. Ardverikie House was built by Sir John in 1873 and is still in use by his family. In ancient times the land belonged to the Cluny Macphersons. The Marquis of Abercorn leased the estate from Cluny Macpherson and entertained Queen Victoria there on her first official visit to the Highlands in 1847. The design is a fairly small Glenurquhart only seven centimetres in the repeat.

ARDVERIKIE

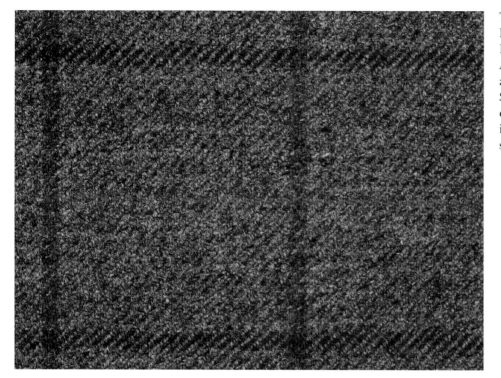

The estate lies on the south side of Loch Earn, thirty miles west of Perth. It has been owned by the Stewarts of Ardvorlich since the sixteenth century and the present owner is Alexander Stewart of Ardvorlich. The tweed was designed by Hunters of Brora and introduced to the estate by the present owner's father about 1965.

ARDVORLICH

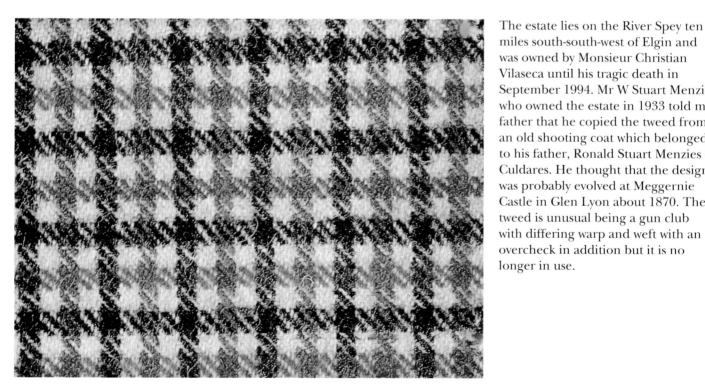

The estate lies on the River Spey ten miles south-south-west of Elgin and was owned by Monsieur Christian Vilaseca until his tragic death in September 1994. Mr W Stuart Menzies who owned the estate in 1933 told my father that he copied the tweed from an old shooting coat which belonged to his father, Ronald Stuart Menzies of Culdares. He thought that the design was probably evolved at Meggernie Castle in Glen Lyon about 1870. The tweed is unusual being a gun club with differing warp and weft with an overcheck in addition but it is no longer in use.

ARNDILLY

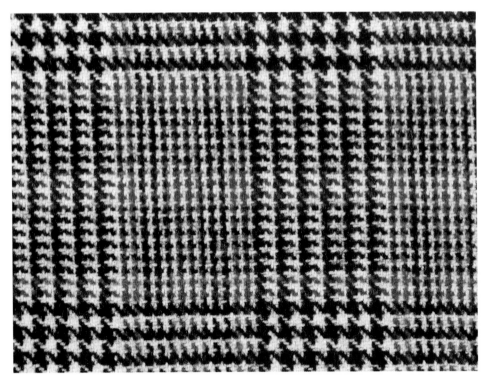

The Atholl estates are in Perthshire ten miles north-west of Pitlochry. They are owned by His Grace, The Duke of Atholl. There is no documentation on this old tweed but Johnstons certainly made it about a hundred and fifty years ago. It is a rather unusual treatment of the Glenurquhart check in the elaborate red overchecking on the 2 and 2 section. It is no longer in use.

OLD ATHOLE OR ATHOLL

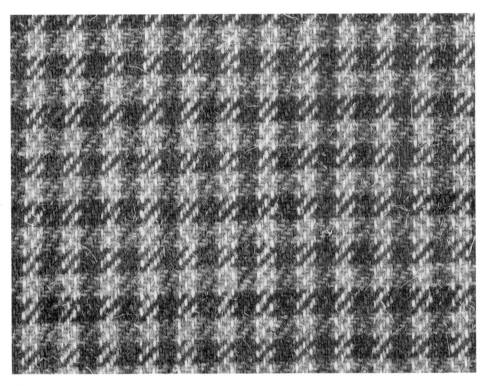

This is a new form of the Atholl check which replaced the older design in 1958. It is a traditional gun club with a combination of white and pale Lovat for the light shades with a stronger Lovat, russet, and a strong mossy tone for the darker colours. The whole effect is very beautiful and is almost invisible on the hill. The original design was made by Haggarts of Aberfeldy.

ATHOLL

The estate lies fifty miles south of Fort William at Bridge of Orchy. It now belongs to Lord Trevor as Auch Estates Limited. Originally Auch was part of the Breadalbane lands and was owned by the Marchioness of Breadalbane. It has since been owned by Mr Tadcastle and Mr Braid Aitken. The design of the tweed comes from Peter MacLennan of Fort William and was introduced around 1974.

AUCH

The estate is some six miles west of Blair Atholl in Perthshire and is owned by Mr D Mackinlay. The tweed was introduced to the estate in its present form in 1965 by Mr I J Mackinlay, there being no record of a previous design and is still in use. The design is one of the group using a plain ground with overchecks.

AUCHLEEKS

Auchnafree lies at the head of Glenalmond some twenty miles west-north-west of Perth. It is owned by the Auchnafree Estate Company and the designer of the tweed, Mrs E J R Whitaker, introduced it to the estate in 1992.

AUCHNAFREE

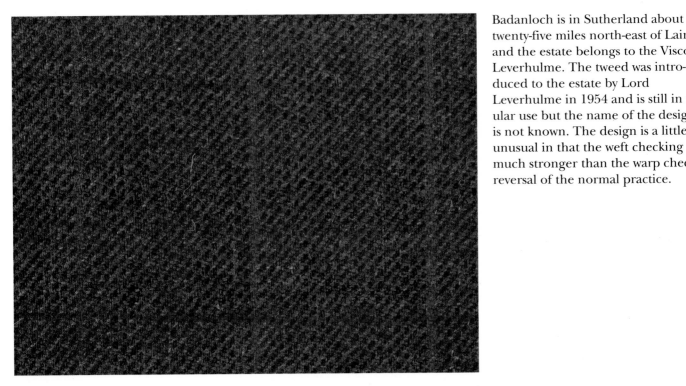

Badanloch is in Sutherland about twenty-five miles north-east of Lairg and the estate belongs to the Viscount Leverhulme. The tweed was introduced to the estate by Lord Leverhulme in 1954 and is still in regular use but the name of the designer is not known. The design is a little unusual in that the weft checking is much stronger than the warp check, a reversal of the normal practice.

BADANLOCH

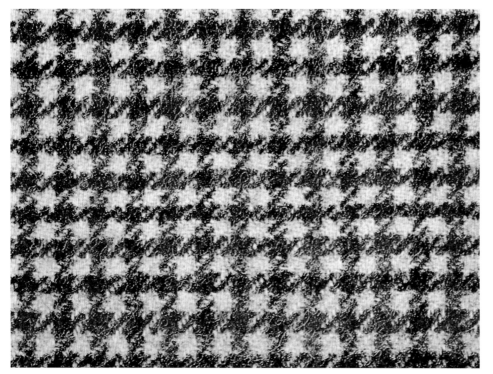

BAILLIE

There is some doubt about the origins of the Baillie. It was used for many years by Lord Burton at the Dochfour Estate on Loch Ness but it has now been replaced there by the Glenquoich. In the old days the Baillies of Dochfour also owned the estate of Eilanreach on the west coast and the pattern may have originated there. In the Johnstons Day Book there is an entry dated 10th November, 1857 for the supply of 'Bailie' but there is nothing to indicate that they were the original makers.

BALAVIL

The estate lies just to the north of Kingussie and belongs to Allan MacPherson-Fletcher of Balavil whose family have owned it since 1780. It was bought then by James MacPherson from the Crown as one of the Forfeited Estates. The tweed was originally a standard design from Hunters of Brora which was later modified a little and introduced to the estate by Mrs MacPherson-Fletcher around 1970. Until 1900 the estate was known as Belleville and it was used as the base for Colonel Thornton's sporting tour of Scotland at the end of the 1790s.

The estate lies about fifteen miles from Elgin just west of south. Ballindalloch was the Strathspey estate of the late Sir Ewan Macpherson-Grant. On his death the title died out and the estate passed to his daughter Clare, who later married Mr Oliver Russell, a cousin of the Duke of Bedford. The tweed which is derived from the Shepherd check with a quiet green overcheck, has varied greatly in tone over the years and is unusual in that the warp and weft light colours are slightly different. The design almost certainly originated in the Johnstons mills at Newmill and is well over a hundred years old. The original design was much redder in tone but the estate now uses this version.

BALLINDALLOCH

The estate of Ballogie lies some five miles south-east of Aboyne in Aberdeenshire on the River Dee. The pattern was introduced in the 1930s by Lt-Colonel R J Nicol, great-uncle of the present owner. It is not known who designed the tweed but it superseded an older design which has not survived. The ground is slightly unusual in being a small herringbone weave.

BALLOGIE

Balmoral lies on the Dee and is the property of Her Majesty, The Queen. Prince Albert designed the Balmoral Tartan sometime before 1857 and the colouring of the tweed is the same. In the Johnstons' records there is an entry showing that 'Super Balmoral Tweed' was woven on 13th July, 1853 but there is no record of the colouring. Perhaps one might speculate whether the tweed or the tartan came first. There were frequent invoices from Johnstons to Macdougalls of Inverness in the 1850s for Balmoral Tweed which makes one think that they sold it as a standard tweed although nowadays its use is strictly confined to the Royal Estate. The ground is a very dark navy and white giving a mid-grey cast with a sprinkling of red spots.

BALMORAL TWEED

This is a true Glenurquhart in construction of very slight contrast and a dull smoky tone. It is checked with one thread of dull gold in the middle of the 2 and 2 part. It was formerly made by Blenkhorn Richardson & Co of Hawick and is not unlike the plain overchecked Lovat also used by the Royal Family. It is not to be reproduced and being strictly confined to the Royal Family is perhaps not really an estate tweed.

BALMORAL LOVAT GLENURQUHART

The estate is near Moulin a little to the east of Pitlochry in Perthshire and is owned by Colonel R Stewart-Wilson, MC. It was designed by Mrs Greville Stewart-Stevens, 10th Lady of Balnakeilly, when she succeeded her uncle Alexander Blair Stewart of Balnakeilly in 1936, and was supplied by Campbells of Beauly. This is a true Glenurquhart, the lighter colour a fawn and the darker a dark reseda-green. There is an overcheck of two threads of soft blue on each side of the 4 and 4 part. The design was once most improperly pirated and was seen being worn by a Member of Parliament at lunch in the Savoy Grill. The laird hopes that this will never happen again.

BALNAKEILLY

This is a tweed on which there is very little hard information. When my father produced his original book he attributed the pattern to 'the west of Sutherland near Shieldaig.' I have been unable to add any more information through my research but the design is old for there is an invoice for it to Macdougalls of Inverness dated 27th July, 1860 and it seems reasonable to suppose that it was originally woven for an estate. While there is no definite proof that Johnstons created the original design this seems likely as the Ing Drab used for the Bateson was one of their special colours.

BATESON

The estate lies at the summit of the Drumochter Pass in Inverness-shire and is owned by Mr and Mrs U Schwarzenbach and Major and Mrs C Hanbury. The tweed was designed by Haggarts of Aberfeldy for Mr P H Byam-Cook, a previous owner, and introduced to the estate in 1967.

BEN ALDER AND DALWHINNIE

The Ben More estate is at the top of the River Oykel about thirty miles south-east of Lochinver, the fishing town on the West Coast. It is owned by the Vestey family trusts who bought the estate from the Godman family in 1982. The design of the tweed is by Hunters of Brora and was introduced by the Vestey family in 1990. It is unusual in having a very complicated system of overchecking with a relatively small repeat of only eight centimetres.

BEN MORE ASSYNT

BEN LOYAL

Ben Loyal is in the north of Sutherland, thirty miles from Lairg. It is owned by Adam, The Count Knuth. It was originally part of the Sutherland estates but was one of the ten estates sold in 1914. In 1939 Loyal was bought by Colonel Douglas Moncreiff and he and his family owned it until 1989 when it was bought by Count Knuth. The Count and Countess designed the first tweed with the head stalker Ian Smart but in 1994 they changed to the second design. The first design is a little unusual in having a herringbone ground with a double overcheck but the second is a Shepherd check derivative with a quiet overcheck.

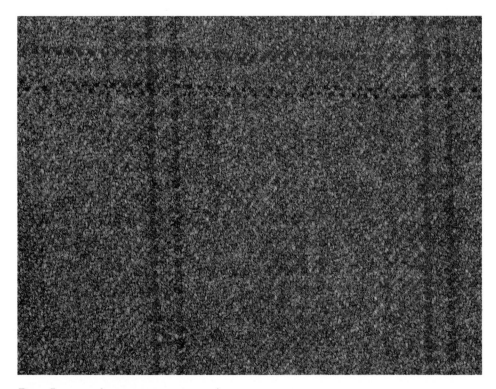

BEN LOYAL (ORIGINAL DESIGN)

The estate lies just south of Glencoe and is owned by Mr Robin Fleming. The Fleming family rented the estate from 1924 to 1935 from Lord Breadalbane and Mr Philip Fleming and his brother-in-law Lord Wyfold bought it from the Breadalbanes in that year. The Breadalbane tweed was greyish and the current tweed was introduced in 1935. The surrounding estates of Glenkinglass, Glenstrae, Glen Etive and Dalness are all owned by the Fleming family and wear the same tweed. The pattern repeat is unusually small being only about four centimetres. (See also Glenkinglass, page 133).

BLACK MOUNT

Blairquhan is six miles south of Maybole in Ayrshire and has been owned by the Hunter Blair family for nearly two hundred years. The tweed was introduced by Sir Edward Hunter Blair, 4th Bart, about 1860, but after some years it fell into disuse. The design was reintroduced by James Hunter Blair, the present owner, who was given a cap by Miss Campbell, daughter of a former head gamekeeper which he had copied. Sadly there is no information on the origins of the original tweed which is a simple gun club.

BLAIRQUHAN

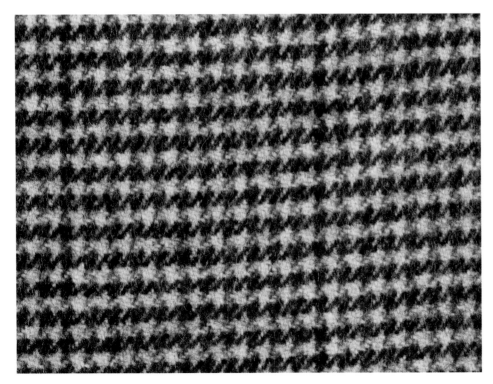

Bolfracks lies to the west of Aberfeldy on the south bank of the River Tay. It belongs to Mr R A Price who inherited the estate from his uncle Mr J D Hutchinson in 1985. It was originally the Home Beat of the Taymouth estate and was bought by Mr Price's grandfather. The tweed was introduced to the estate by Mr Hutchinson who designed it with Haggarts of Aberfeldy.

BOLFRACKS

Boreland is in Glenlochay, the River Lochay runs into the southern end of Loch Tay, five miles south-west of Aberfeldy. It belongs to Judge R A R Stroyan QC and the tweed which was designed by Haggarts of Aberfeldy was introduced to the estate by Judge Stroyan's father in 1947.

BORELAND

The estate lies in Glen Strathfarrar about twelve miles slightly south of west from Inverness. It is owned by Andras Limited. The tweed was designed and introduced by the present owners with the help of Campbells of Beauly. Braulen originally formed part of the Lovat estates and was purchased by its current owners in 1990.

BRAULEN

This is one of the oldest patterns on the Johnstons list but it has no traceable history and I have really included it in the hope that some reader may be able to shed some light on its origin. The design comes in the middle of a group of estate tweeds in an old Johnstons pattern book of the 1870s which would indicate that it belonged to some estate. It bears a startling resemblance to the Mamore, both in colour and in the unusual arrangement of the single red threads of the overchecking. The Kintail is another very similar design which uses the single red thread to outline the overcheck.

THE BROOK

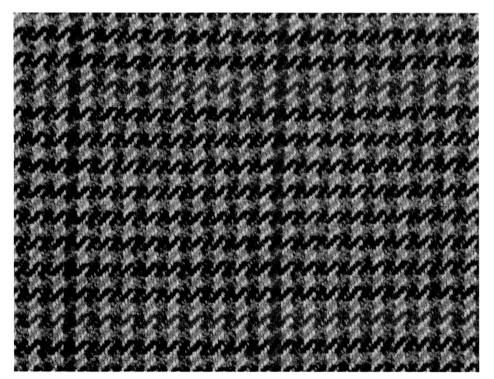

CAMUSERICHT

Camusericht lies on the 'Road to the Isles' at the west end of Loch Rannoch on the north shore. Loch Rannoch is twenty-five miles west of Pitlochry and the estate belongs to Mr and Mrs L H Kerfoot. There is no information on the tweed, who designed it or when but it is basically an overchecked Shepherd.

CAMUSRORY

The estate lies at the head of the sea loch, Loch Nevis, which is five miles or so east of Mallaig. The tweed was designed by the late Colonel, Sir Oliver Crosthwaite-Eyre and was originally used on the Knoydart estate of which Camusrory forms a part. It was reintroduced to Camusrory in 1993 when the Crosthwaite-Eyre family bought the estate from Mr R Wadsworth. Camusrory is reached by sea down Loch Nevis, the alternative being a six mile walk from Mallaig.

The estate of Candacraig lies in Donside about fifty miles west of Aberdeen and is in trust for the two sons of the present Laird Mr F A Wallace. The tweed design was introduced by Mr A F Wallace in 1890 and was slightly varied in 1950 by A L P F Wallace. Over the years the colours have varied a little, as in all the old estate tweeds, and the present version is much lighter in tone so that the twilled effect of the 1968 version is much less marked.

CANDACRAIG

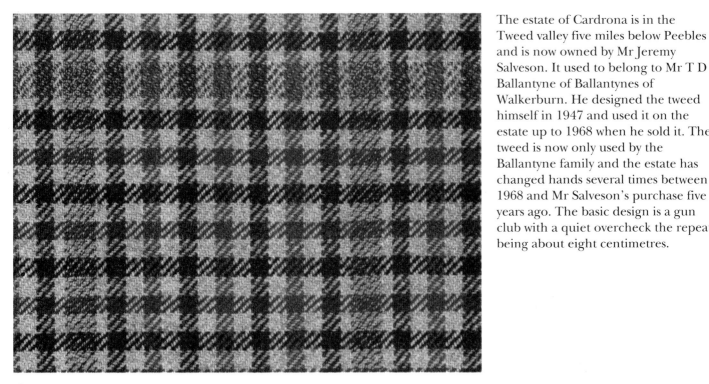

The estate of Cardrona is in the Tweed valley five miles below Peebles and is now owned by Mr Jeremy Salveson. It used to belong to Mr T D Ballantyne of Ballantynes of Walkerburn. He designed the tweed himself in 1947 and used it on the estate up to 1968 when he sold it. The tweed is now only used by the Ballantyne family and the estate has changed hands several times between 1968 and Mr Salveson's purchase five years ago. The basic design is a gun club with a quiet overcheck the repeat being about eight centimetres.

CARDRONA

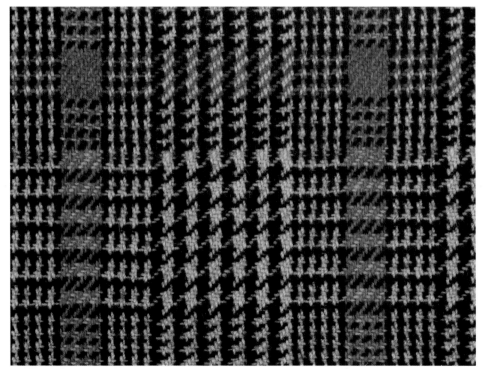

THE CARNEGIE

The Carnegie is used on the estate of Southesk which lies a little to the south-east of Brechin. The estate is held by the Southesk Settlement, a Carnegie family trust, and is the home of the Earl of Southesk, son of the Duke of Fife who is the head of the Carnegie family. The design is a straightforward Glenurquhart but the handling of the overcheck is unusual. It is not known who designed the tweed but the first firm date is in a pattern book of George Harrison of Edinburgh of 1902. It is believed that the tweed was introduced by the 9th Earl and the Earl of Northesk, another branch of the family, around 1880. Andrew Carnegie the great philanthropist was photographed wearing the tweed in 1908.

CARNOUSIE

The estate is on the Deveron river near Turriff in Aberdeenshire but there is no information on who designed the tweed or when it was introduced. It is a true Glenurquhart with the red guarding overcheck on the alternate basses of the 4 and 4 making a fairly large repeat of about fourteen centimetres. It is probably the darkest of the estate tweeds.

Castle Fraser used to be owned by Major Michael Smiley and this simple Lovat with a double check of gold-brown twist was adopted in 1947 by Mrs M Smiley and was supplied by Russells of Insch in Aberdeenshire. Castle Fraser is one of the finest in Scotland and is part of the 'castle tour' of Aberdeenshire. It is three miles from Monymusk and its old name was the Castle of Muchal in Mar. It is unlikely that the tweed is still used on the estate as the castle is now the property of the National Trust.

CASTLE FRASER

Cawdor estate and its castle of Macbeth fame lies inland about six miles south-west of Nairn which is on the Moray Firth. It is owned by the 6th Earl of Cawdor who designed and introduced the tweed in 1980. It is still used on the estate. The pattern is a slightly unusual variant of the gun club as the red crossing of the weft is not repeated in the warp.

CAWDOR

COIGACH

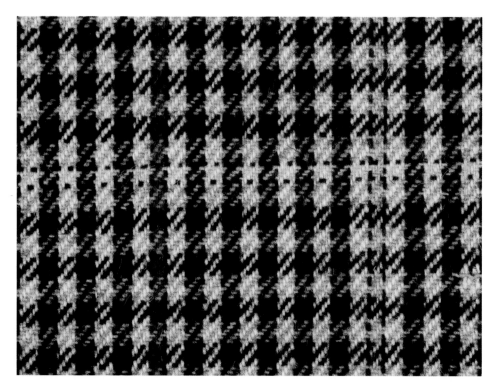

CEANNACROC

The estate and area of Coigach lie just north-west of Ullapool on the west coast. It was part of the lands of the Earls of Cromartie until 1950 when it was sold to the Henman and Longstaff families with the Coigach Salmon Fishings being sold separately. There is no information on who designed the tweed nor even whether it was used on the estate but it seems likely. Johnstons first invoiced the tweed to Macdougalls of Inverness on 3rd November, 1846 and went on to make it in much greater quantities than could be used by one estate. The present Earl of Cromartie suggested that it might have been used on the Sutherland estates as there was a connection by marriage between the two families. It is one of the great seminal designs not only of the estate tweeds but of the whole textile trade. The design was adopted about 1874 by one of the gun clubs in the United States although the exact club remains unknown. Perhaps because the original name is hard to pronounce the name 'gun club' stuck and this class of tweed design is now known as a gun club throughout the world.

Ceannacroc lies at the east end of Loch Cluanie some fifteen miles west of Fort Augustus. It is owned by Mr Martin Girvan. There is, unfortunately, no information on the origins of the tweed which is no longer used on the estate. It is a slightly unusual variant of the Shepherd check as it uses different light colours in the warp and weft, although they may at one time have been the same. A double system of overchecks makes an exceptionally long repeat of about twenty centimetres. Bonnie Prince Charlie is supposed to have lived in a cave in the Ceannacroc hills after the '45.

Conaglen originally formed part of the Ardgour Estates a few miles north of Fort William. It was bought by the Morton family who are thought to have introduced the tweed some time before 1956 when the estate passed to the present owner Mr J Guthrie and his family. The tweed was designed by Hunters of Brora.

CONAGLEN

The estate of Corrour lies in the middle of Rannoch Moor fifteen miles to the east of Ben Nevis and for many years was only reachable by train. It is owned by the Maxwell Macdonald family. The patterns were introduced by Sir John Stirling-Maxwell around 1900 and were first made at the mill at Kilmahog near Callander. The tweed is now no longer used on the hill as it was found to be insufficiently hard-wearing and a standard production tweed is used instead. There is no information why there were two patterns originally but they were nearly invisible on the hill at Corrour.

CORROUR NOS 1 & 2

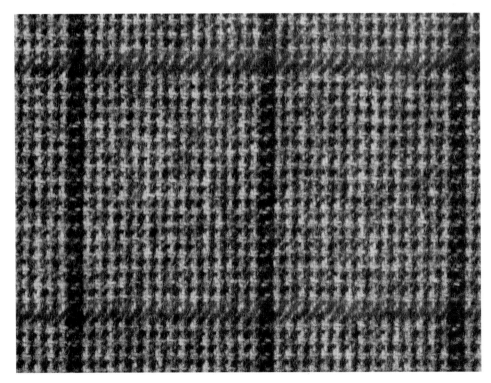

The estate lies on Rannoch Moor some forty miles due west of Pitlochry and is owned by Lord Pearson of Rannoch. The estate used to be stalked from Black Corries Lodge in Glencoe but is now stalked from Rannoch Barracks at the west end of Loch Rannoch. The tweed in use, which was one of three differing grounds, was introduced in 1968 and was probably designed by Haggarts of Aberfeldy.

CRUACH

This is quite one of the boldest of the estate checks and is simply the Coigach multiplied by two. Each check is three-eighths of an inch wide and while it would make a most conspicuous pattern walking down Prince's Street in Edinburgh it would be fairly inconspicuous on the hill. As my father wrote in 1968 there is no information on this tweed. Johnstons first invoiced it to Macdougalls of Inverness on 24th June, 1871 and it is likely that it was intended for some estate although the name seems a curious one. In this respect it is like the Bateson. The Dacres were a well known Border family and possibly the tweed is connected with them.

DACRE

DALHOUSIE

The estates of the Earl of Dalhousie lie ten miles north-west of Montrose. The estates of Edzell, Brechin and Invermark use the tweed. There are two illustrations of the Dalhousie, the original from the 1968 book and the one in use at the present, showing how, over the years, a change or changes of maker can affect the appearance of the design. The weft check is almost invisible in the new version. The warp repeat, which does not show in the illustration, is about eleven centimetres. The ground design of a broken herringbone is most unusual.

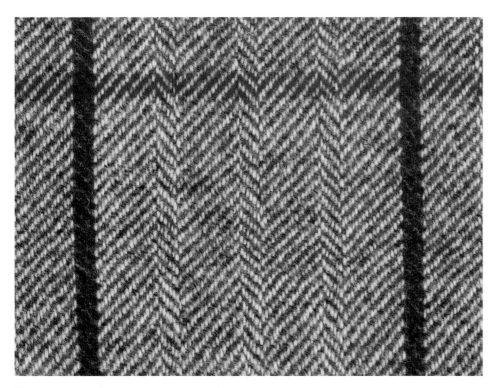

DALHOUSIE (ORIGINAL DESIGN)

Delgatie Castle and estate are just beside Turriff and are owned by Captain John Hay of Delgatie who is Chief of Clan Hay. Perhaps these two patterns are strictly speaking Clan Hay tweeds but as they are used on the estate they qualify as estate tweeds. There is no information on when they were developed or who designed them but they are both gun clubs with a red overcheck. In the idiom of the tartans the brown version is the hunting one. The white version appears in Johnstons pattern books of over a century ago as both Hay and Dupplin. The Dupplin tweed is an enlarged version of the Delgatie.

DELGATIE (BROWN VERSION)

DELGATIE (WHITE VERSION)

Delnabo lies a mile to the west of Tomintoul and is owned by the Yeowart family who bought it in 1990. It was part of the Grant-Seafield estates until 1891 when it was bought by Mr J G Smith. It is not known who designed or introduced the tweed but it is still in use on the estate which has extensive historical records.

DELNABO

The estate lies between Aboyne and Ballater to the north of the River Dee. It is owned by Mr E C M Humphrey. The tweed was designed and introduced between the wars by Mr A Duley-Hamilton. It is a fairly small Glenurquhart but the repeat is every twelve centimetres because the overchecking is on every alternate block of the 4 and 4.

DINNET

The estate is bounded on the north side by the River Spey and is close to Grantown-on-Spey. It is owned by Lady Pauline Ogilvie Grant Nicholson. The tweed was designed and introduced by Lady Pauline about 1970. Dorback has always been a Seafield estate and Lady Pauline inherited it on the death of her mother, Nina, Countess of Seafield. The design is a Shepherd check with overcheck, the ground check is varied by a slight difference in the depth of the dark colour in warp and weft.

DORBACK AND REVACK

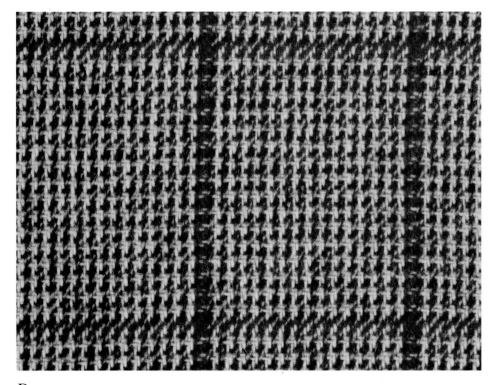

Dougarie is on the west coast of the Isle of Arran and belongs to Mr S C Gibbs. The estate was bought by Mr Gibbs from Lady Mary Boscawen in 1972. Originally as far back as the 1500s Dougarie belonged to the Dukes of Hamilton. It was inherited by the Duchess of Montrose and passed to Lady Mary. The present tweed was designed by Haggarts of Aberfeldy and introduced by Mr Gibbs in 1974

DOUGARIE

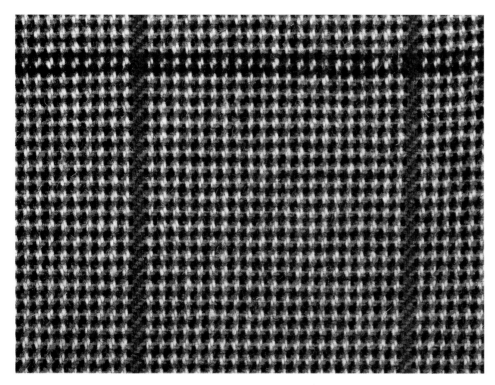

The estate lies some six miles north of Auchterarder and belongs to Baroness Willoughby de Eresby. The purple warp check is a little unusual as is the effect of the light spot on the 2 and 2 in the centre of the crimson weft check. There is no information on who designed the tweed which was introduced in the first part of the twentieth century and is known as the Glenartney Tweed. It is worn by the stalkers and keepers on the hill area of the Drummond Estate which is centred in the medieval forest of Glenartney.

DRUMMOND

The estate lies about twenty-four miles south of Wick and belongs to Mr R Stanton Avery who bought it in 1967 from Mr H Blyth. In previous times the estate formed part of the Sinclair lands and in 1650, as part of his campaign to put down the Covenanters, James Graham, Marquis of Montrose besieged Dunbeath Castle. The tweed was designed by Hunters of Brora and introduced by Mr Avery in 1985.

DUNBEATH

The estate is on the north-east coast of Islay running south for about ten miles from Port Askaig. The estate is owned by Mr B L Schroder and it is thought that the design was introduced in the 1920s. At that time the Islay Woollen Mills were let to Mr J T Christie and it is assumed that he was the designer. It is a simple pattern with a fairly bold red overcheck and a very quiet blue one which tends to sink into the ground colouring.

DUNLOSSIT

Dunecht is twelve miles to the west of Aberdeen and is owned by Lord Cowdray. The pattern is a straightforward gun club and was introduced to the estate by Annie, 1st Viscountess Cowdray in February 1927. It seems probable that she was the designer. The tweed is sometimes called The Cowdray.

DUNECHT

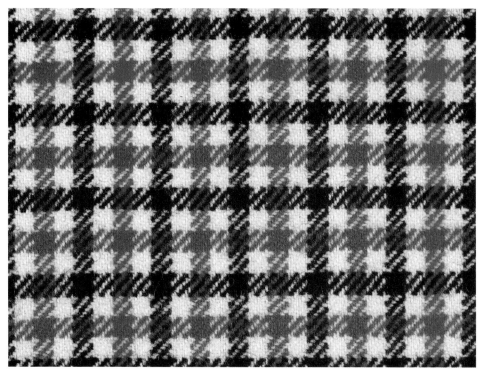

DUPPLIN OR HAY

Dupplin Castle, the ancient stronghold of the Hay Clan just west of Perth, was sold by the Earl of Kinnoul to Mr John Dewar in 1911 and Mr Dewar was created Lord Forteviot in 1916. The castle still belongs to Lord Forteviot. This tweed is allied to the Delgatie and in 1968 Captain Hay suggested to my father that the name be changed to Delgatie. As can be seen the tweeds are exactly similar except for the size of the pattern. I have retained the original name as the pattern has been on the Johnstons lists at Elgin for more than one hundred and fifty years. It is no longer used on the Dupplin estate.

EDRADYNATE

The estate is on the north bank of the River Tay about three miles north-east of Aberfeldy. It is the property of Mr Michael Campbell who bought it from Major David Gibson in 1983. Before that Edradynate had belonged to the Stewarts for five hundred years from 1465. Mr Campbell introduced the tweed to the estate with Haggarts of Aberfeldy in 1984. The quiet chrome-coloured stripe between the red stripes tends to sink into the ground colour. The bold red stripes represent Breadalbane. Mr Campbell is a Loudon Campbell and the Loudons were a sept of the Breadalbanes.

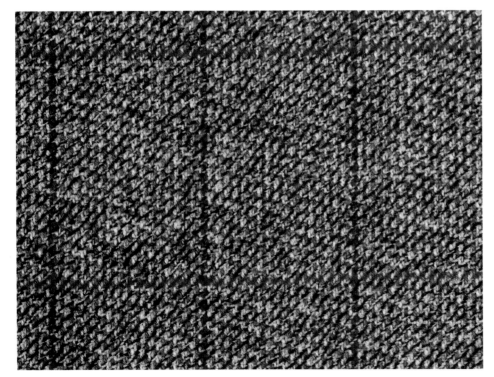

Castle Erchless is on the River Beauly to the west of Inverness and the estate covers a great area of mountainous country. It is owned by The Hon Maurice Robson. It was originally a Chisholm estate and was sold to Baron Stackelberg in 1935 and then to Sir Lawrence Robson in 1962. The original tweed had no overchecking and was slightly yellower in tone than the present. It was presumably designed by the Chisholms as Johnstons invoiced it to Macdougalls of Inverness in August 1852. There is no information on who designed the present tweed but it is like the Gannochy and Glencanisp (designed by Hunters of Brora) the difference lying in the colour of the overcheck.

ERCHLESS

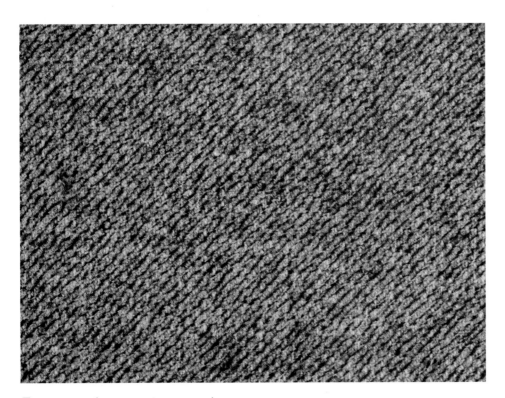

ERCHLESS (ORIGINAL DESIGN)

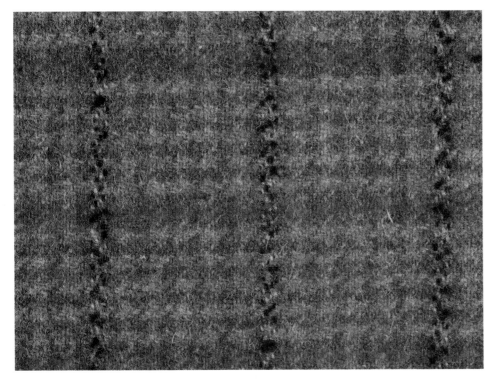

EILANREACH

Eilanreach lies on the Sound of Sleat on the mainland just opposite the Isle of Skye near Glenelg. It is owned by Lord Dulverton and was purchased by his father in 1947. The tweed was designed around 1950 by Lord and Lady Dulverton and Sir John MacLeod who owned the Cuchulin Handloom Company. Originally the estate was owned by the Baillies of Dochfour and was rented for a number of years at the turn of the century by the Master of Blantyre. The estate was then sold to the Scott family from the Hill of Nigg who in turn sold it to the Dulvertons in 1947. The tweed is unusual in having a bold black and yellow twist for its warp overcheck element.

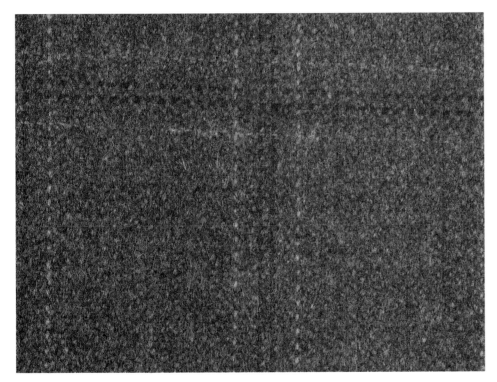

ESSLEMONT

Esslemont lies slightly west of Ellon fifteen miles north of Aberdeen and is owned by Charles Wolrige Gordon. It has been in the family since 1720. Before 1720 the family seat was at Hallhead adjoining Craigievar but when the Laird went bankrupt he was bought out by his younger brother who had made a fortune in claret in Bordeaux. At the same time he bought Esslemont. He and his eldest son were ardent Jacobites, the latter being greatly involved in the '45 rebellion. After the '45 he went into exile in France where he died and the estates were forfeited to the Crown. The estates were returned to the family in 1760 when the eldest son returned from France. The tweed was designed by Captain Robert Wolrige Gordon and his wife. It was introduced in 1967.

The estate is five miles west of Muir of Ord in Ross-shire. It is owned by Mr Roderick Stirling and the tweed was introduced about 1925 by his father Major Sir John Stirling, KT, MBE. It was made by A & J Macnab of Slateford near Edinburgh.

FAIRBURN

Fannich lies to the east of Loch Maree in Ross and Cromarty about twenty miles south of Ullapool. It belongs to Baron W van Dedem. Mr Vernon Watney bought the estate in 1900 and is said to have introduced the tweed but Johnstons invoiced it to Macdougalls of Inverness as far back as 3rd July, 1860. There is, however, no evidence to show who designed it and Johnstons may not even have been the first makers. The estate was subsequently sold to Mr T W Sandeman who then sold it to Baron W van Dedem in 1976.

FANNICH

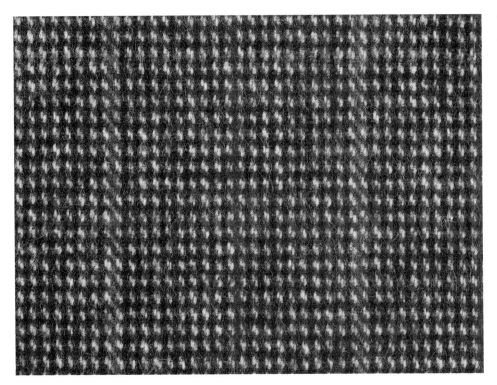

The estate lies just north-west of Aberfeldy in Perthshire and belongs to Mr Nicholas Fane. It originally belonged to Major N G Ramsay who designed and introduced the tweed in 1955 as the maker of the previous tweed had gone out of business. The estate, less the original house and policies, was bought by the Fane family in 1988 together with the right to wear the tweed which is still in use on the estate. The estate house is now The Manse at Weem near Aberfeldy.

FARLEYER

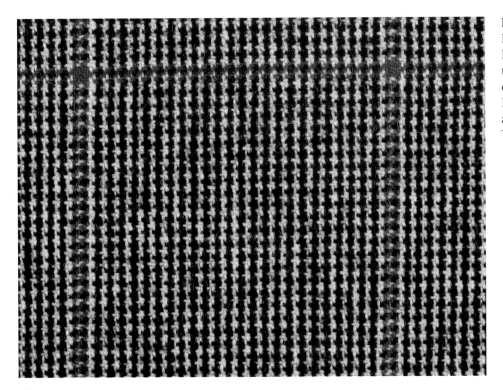

Farr lies ten miles to the south of Inverness and belongs to Major C D Mackenzie of Farr House. He believes that the tweed was probably introduced to the estate by the late Austin Mackenzie of Carradale, around 1900 and who may well have designed it. This is not certain.

FARR

The estate lies in the Feugh Valley near Aboyne and has been owned by the Farquharsons of Finzean for sixteen generations, the current owners being Donald and Andrew of that Ilk. The grouse moor on the estate was first let in 1840. The estate tweed was introduced by the family in 1964 and the design was a modification of a tweed created by Mr Tom Simpson of Hunters of Brora. The repeat is fairly large, about twelve centimetres and the gold lines are a stripe, not repeated in the weft.

FINZEAN

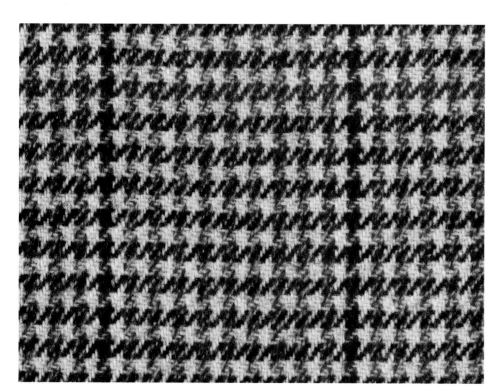

The estate is ten miles south-west of Berwick and is owned by the 5th Lord Joicey. Strictly speaking it is an English estate but while not really part of what were known as the Debatable Lands, owing to the south-westerly direction of the Border, it is only three miles from it. The name of the designer is not known but the tweed was introduced by the 1st Lord Joicey about 1920. The Scottish connection is underlined as the tweed is made by Haggarts of Aberfeldy. As a checked Shepherd it is slightly unusual as the weft checking is lighter than the ground and therefore the warp check has a striped effect.

FORD AND ETAL

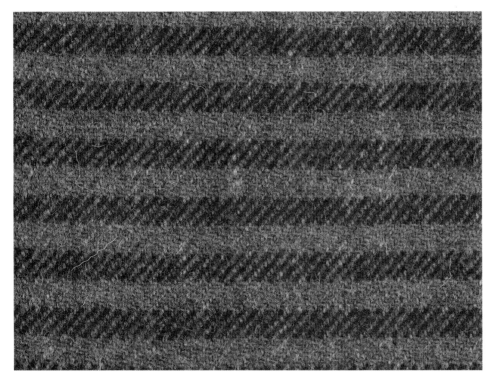

The estate is near Turriff in Aberdeenshire and while the castle is now the property of the National Trust for Scotland, the estate is still in the hands of the Forbes-Leith family. The tweed was certainly introduced as far back as 1889, possibly earlier, but there is no evidence who designed it. As protective colouring in the area it is ideal.

FYVIE

This pattern comes from the area of Gairloch in Wester Ross and perhaps its claim to a place in this book may be a little doubtful. Johnstons first invoiced the pattern to Macdougalls of Inverness on 15th July, 1846 and it seem reasonable to suppose that it was for the Gairloch estate. It is almost an exact copy of the Coigach, the dark colours are identical, but in the weft the white ground is replaced with a yellow and white twist. This slight alteration gives a much warmer effect to the pattern as a whole.

GAIRLOCH

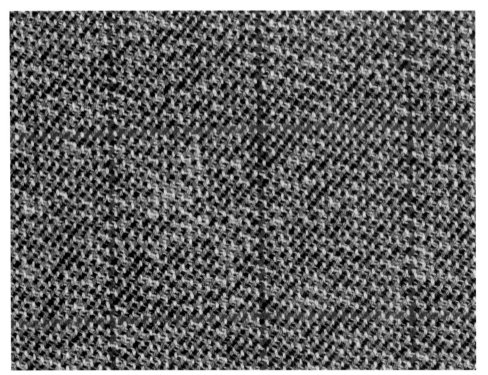

Gannochy is in Angus about ten miles north of Brechin and is owned by Mr and Mrs D H Ruttenberg. It was originally part of the Dalhousie estates and the original tweed was very like the Dalhousie tweed but with a purple overcheck. The estate was sold to William Foster in 1961 and the present owners bought it in 1981. They designed the current tweed in 1983. It is not unlike the Erchless and the Glencanisp, the difference lies in the colouring of the overchecking.

GANNOCHY

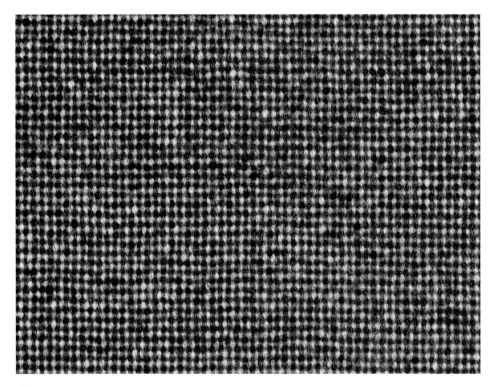

Garden is owned by Mr James Stirling of Garden and is in Stirlingshire at Buchlyvie. The tweed was designed by Colonel Archibald Stirling of Garden and Sir John Stirling-Maxwell to be a derivative of the Corrour. The Garden tweed is unique amongst Scottish estate tweeds in being more like an Irish Donegal than a Scottish cloth. It is what is known in the weaving trade as a 'plain cloth' with one thread of black and one of white in the warp being crossed with a tawny yellow in the weft.

GARDEN

Glenample is at the western end of Loch Earn on the south side, thirty miles west of Perth. It was bought by Senor Raphael Cruz Conde, the present owner from Mr D Abbot in 1992 and before that Mr Abbot bought it from the Stirlings of Keir in 1988. Senor Cruz Conde designed the tweed with Haggarts of Aberfeldy and introduced it in 1994.

GLENAMPLE

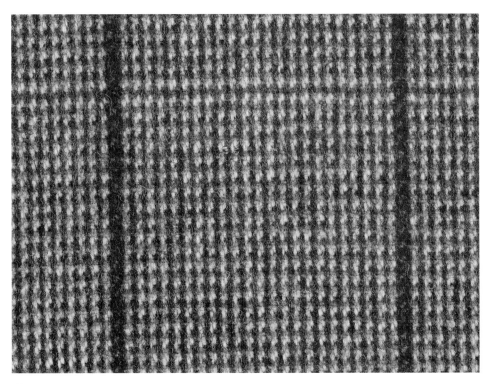

Glenavon is in the Cairngorms twenty miles or so east of Aviemore and is owned by Sir Seton and Lady Wills. The design for the tweed came from Meggernie Castle in Glen Lyon, Meggernie's green warp being replaced by a dark crimson, and the tweed was introduced by Major G S Wills in 1963. Before 1935 the estate belonged to the Duke of Richmond and Gordon who sold it to Colonel Oliver Haigh.

GLENAVON

NORTH GLENBUCHAT

SOUTH GLENBUCHAT

The estates of North and South Glenbuchat are in Aberdeenshire where the Water of Buchat joins the River Don. Until 1969 they were one estate bought by Mr James W Barclay in 1901. The northern part was sold to Lord Cowdray and The Hon Mrs Lavinia Smiley in 1969 and sold again to Mr D W F Tulloch in 1981. Mrs Barclay Sole, granddaughter of Mr James Barclay, and her son retain the southern part. The estate tweeds were commissioned by Mrs Sole's father and the only difference in them is the colour of the overcheck. The South Glenbuchat tweed is no longer used on the estate but the North Glenbuchat is. There is an excellent local history called *The Book of Glenbuchat.*

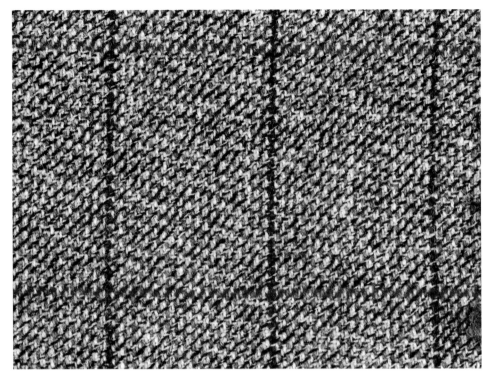

The estate lies just to the east of Lochinver on the west coast. It was once part of the Sutherland estates but has been owned by the Vestey family since 1936. The design, like the Ben More Assynt tweed, is by Hunters of Brora and was introduced by the Vestey family in 1990. The tweed is like the Gannochy and the Erchless, the differences lying in the overchecking colouring.

GLENCANISP

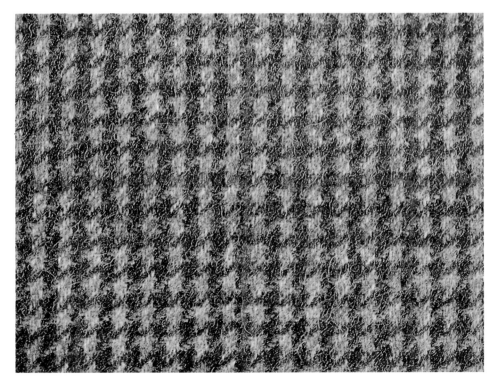

This attractive and quiet tweed is used on two estates Glendelvine and Riemore in the Dunkeld district of Perthshire. Both estates have belonged to the Lyle family for generations and are now owned by Sir Gavin Lyle, Bt (Glendelvine) and Lt Colonel A M Lyle (Riemore).
The pattern was introduced by Sir Alexander Lyle, Bt about 1920 and was made by Hunters of Brora. It is a simple Shepherd check in browns with a very quiet overcheck.

GLENDELVINE AND RIEMORE

GLENDOE

Glendoe lies on the south side of Loch Ness near Fort Augustus and belongs to the Vernon family through Hillhouse Estates Limited. There are two estate tweeds. The first is the one in use at the present, designed by Hunters of Brora and introduced by the Vernons in 1993. The second pattern was given to my father by Campbells of Beauly in 1967 but there was no information on where the tweed came from nor who designed it. In the 1870s Glendoe was part of the Lovat lands and was acquired by Major M S B Vernon from Major J Godman in 1957. Between the wars it was owned for a number of years by the Hambro family.

GLENDOE (ORIGINAL DESIGN)

Fasque lies six miles north-west of Laurencekirk on the Forfar-Aberdeen road. Glen Dye is to the north. At present the estate is owned by Mr Charles Gladstone and it has been in his family for over a hundred and fifty years. There is no information on exactly when the tweed was introduced but the Gladstone family probably designed it.

GLEN DYE AND FASQUE

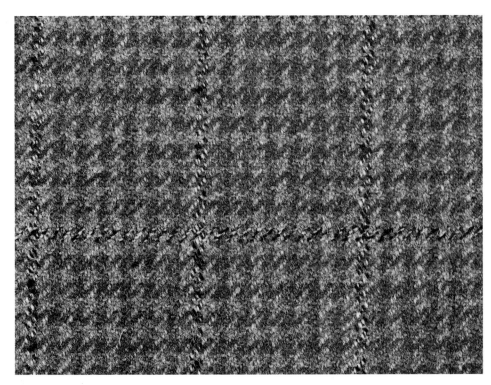

Glenfeshie lies ten miles or so south of Aviemore. It was owned by Mr J M F Dibben who bought it from West Highland Woodlands in 1987. Lord Dulverton introduced the tweed when he took over the estate in 1967 but the designer is not known. The pattern is a simple Shepherd check with an unusual marled overcheck. The original Glenfeshie tweed designed by Miss Balfour can be seen under Aberchalder (page 88). In 1994 the estate of Glenfeshie was bought by the Wills Woodland Trust but there is no information on whether the tweed will continue in use.

GLENFESHIE

GLENFINNAN

Glenfinnan is at the head of Loch Shiel, west of Fort William, where the monument commemorates the gathering of the clans at the start of the 1745 rebellion. The estate is owned by Mr M R Warren. The design was introduced by Macdonald of Glenalladale some time between 1910 and 1930. The land around Glenfinnan is unusually sandy coloured and bright though the tweed appears it blends in admirably on the hill.

GLENISLA

The estate lies beside Cortachy, a village about eight miles north-west of Forfar and is the property of Lord Airlie. There is no definite information on who designed the tweed but Lord Airlie thinks it may have been his great-grandmother Blanche, Countess of Airlie who introduced it to the estate about 1880. It has been used on the estate ever since. The design is a Glenurquhart in brown and white, differing in size from the true Glenurquhart and, except for the colour, similar to the Green Mar.

Glenkinglass is on the eastern shore of Loch Etive about fifteen miles from Oban. It was originally owned by the Marquess of Breadalbane and was bought by the first Baron Wyfold in 1935. Lord Wyfold who designed and introduced the tweed in 1936 was the father of the present owner The Hon, Mrs L F Schuster. The owners of the neighbouring estates Dalness, Glen Etive and Black Mount are cousins of Mrs Schuster and use the same tweed. Under Black Mount (page 103) is shown the pattern in use in 1967 which is slightly darker and slightly squatter in the check.

GLENKINGLASS

Properly Glenlivet is three estates, part of the Richmond and Gordon Speyside estates taken over by the Crown in lieu of death duties in the 1930s; Glenlivet, Strathavon and Lecht. They lie to the north of Tomintoul. The shootings were acquired by Major Richard Waddington about 1947 when he and Mr Peter Saunders designed and introduced the tweed for the keepers. The tweed is not just confined to those who work on the estate but is also available to visiting shooting parties. Because of the elaborate overchecking it has a repeat of about sixteen centimetres.

GLENLIVET

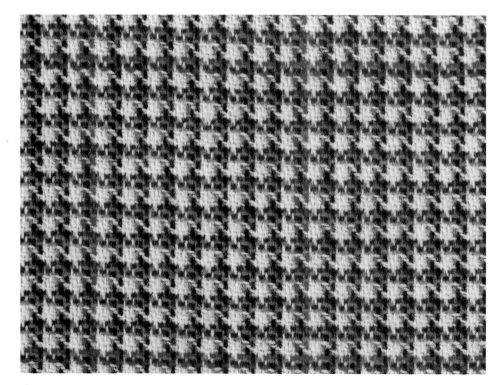

GLENMOIDART

Glenmoidart lies on the west of Loch Shiel twenty miles from Fort William. It is owned by Mrs Lees-Millais. There is no evidence on when the tweed was introduced to the estate nor who designed it. The design is unusual in that the ground weave is a small diamond and not the usual twill.

GLEN MORISTON

As the crow flies Glen Moriston is five miles north-west of Fort Augustus. The glen starts at Invermoriston on Loch Ness and the estate belonged to the Grant family for nearly six hundred years. In the late 1980s part of the estate was sold off and fragmented but a portion and the house were retained by the Grants. The tweed is one of the oldest estate tweeds there is and first appears in the Johnstons sales book on 22nd July, 1851. It may have been adopted by Caroline, Countess of Seafield as her estate of Glen Urquhart lies immediately to the east. The design was extensively adopted by the tweed trade in the late 19th century. It was found to be too bright for use on the hill and it was replaced in the twentieth century by stock tweeds from Campbells of Beauly.

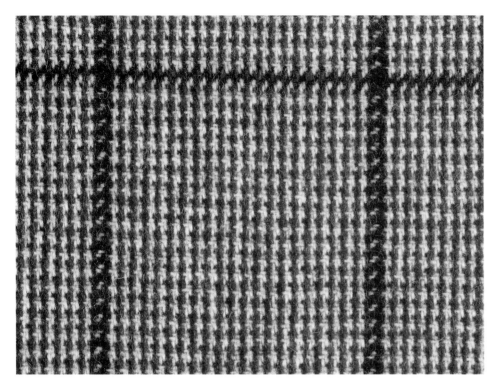

Glenmuick is just south of the River Dee at Ballater. The tweed was introduced to the estate by the Mackenzie family who owned it in the nineteenth century. Its use was continued by the Walker-Okeover family who bought the estate from the Mackenzies in 1948. The estate is now owned by Sir Peter Walker-Okeover.

GLENMUICK

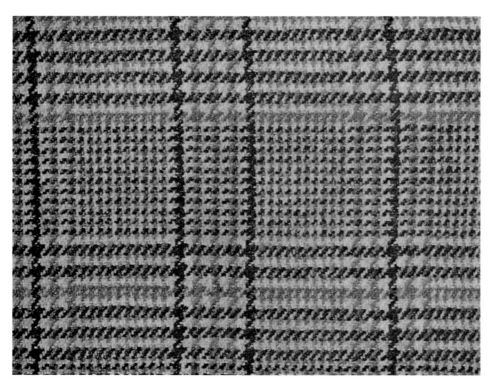

Glen Orchy is in Argyllshire near Dalmally about thirty miles south-east of Fort William. It now belongs to Forest Enterprise. It once belonged to the Campbells of Breadalbane but was sold to Sir Douglas Montgomery Hall in 1936 and then to the late Captain Oldham in 1946. Forest Enterprise bought the estate in 1967. The tweed is now no longer in use but it is unusually colourful and there may have been a Shepherd check type in the same colours as the Glenurquhart version illustrated.

GLEN ORCHY

GLENOGIL

Glenogil lies about eight miles north of Forfar and belongs to the Earl of Woolton. The Woolton Trustees bought the estate from Lord Woolton's stepfather, the late Lord Forres in 1974 and continued to use the estate tweed. The original tweed was designed by Lord Forres and the Strathmore Woollen Company but around 1970 this was replaced by the current tweed which was designed by Hunters of Brora.

GLENOGIL (ORIGINAL DESIGN)

GLEN QUOICH

Glen Quoich is in the north-west Highlands twenty miles west from Fort Augustus and has one of the highest recorded annual rainfalls in the British Isles. It is owned by the Gordon family of Lude near Blair Atholl, and the Burton Property Trustees who own the east beat along with the neighbouring forests of Cluanie and Glen Shiel. Lord Burton uses this tweed for all his estates. It was first introduced by the current Lord Burton's great-grandfather who may have designed it.

GLENSANDA

The estate which includes Kingairloch, lies on the Morvern Peninsula in North Argyll. Originally it formed part of the territory of the Macleans of Kingairloch but a gambling debt of £11,000 forced the family to sell to James Forbes in 1800. In 1902 the estate was bought by George Herbert Strutt of Belper, Derbyshire, great-great- grandson of Jebediah Strutt who was the co-founder with Sir Richard Arkwright of the cotton spinning trade in Great Britain. The estate was sold to the present owner, Mrs Angela Yeoman, OBE of Foster Yeoman Ltd, in 1982. The tweed was introduced in 1984 and is based on an old estate pattern.

GLEN TANAR

The estate lies four miles to the south-west of Aboyne on Deeside and is now owned by Miss Claire M Bruce of Glen Tanar House. The pattern was probably introduced around 1912 by the first Lord Glentanar and it has proved an effective camouflage on the hill. Miss Bruce has sent a pattern of a lighter weight worsted cloth which is also used on the estate and which is reproduced as well. While the basic pattern remains the same, though smaller, the variation in depth of colour is dramatic.

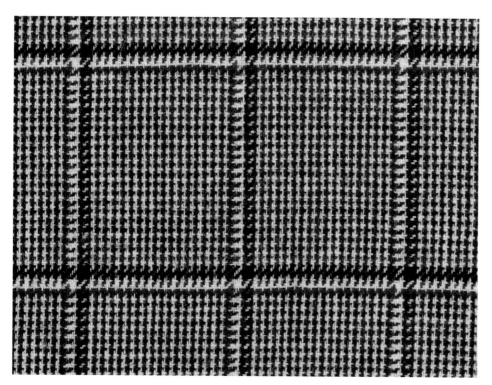

GLEN TANAR (LIGHTWEIGHT PATTERN)

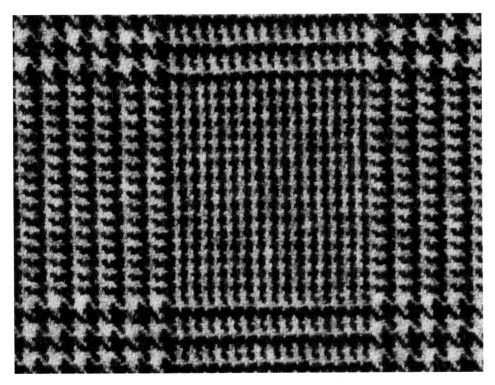

GLENURQUHART

The Glenurquhart is one of the small list of outstanding designs which has influenced fashion houses all over the world. It was adopted by Caroline, Countess of Seafield for her estates about 1840. The story has it that the design was created by Elizabeth Macdougall of Lewiston and is a combination of a portion of the Shepherd and another pattern woven two of black and two of white, approximately two inches of each. The designer had great difficulty in getting William Fraser, the weaver, to understand her instructions and she sketched the pattern in the mud at the cottage door. The design was originally dark blue and white but was later changed to the black and white that we see today. Interestingly enough in the Day Book of Johnstons for June, 1851 there is an invoice for a web of Glenurquhart for Macdougalls of Inverness and in the

same month a web of Coigach and a web of Glen Moriston for the same customer. Glen Moriston is the next glen to the west of Glen Urquhart and was also part of the Seafield estates. This invoice suggests that the original pattern may have been created early in the 1840s for Glenurquhart was originally woven commercially at the mill at Drumnadrochit and from there the manufacture moved to Inverness. It is not unreasonable to assume that it might have taken ten years to get from William Fraser's narrow loom in the west to the more sophisticated broadlooms of Johnstons.
The Drumnadrochit mill closed down early in the 1950s and was then used as a house. The mill was one of the first attempts to introduce industry to the Highlands after the '45 and was built by the Laird of Grant at the same time as the Honourable

Commissioners for the Annexed Estates built the mill at Invermoriston close by. The lists of the women to whom the King's Commissioners distributed spinning wheels to supply yarn to the mills can be found in the archives of Castle Grant.

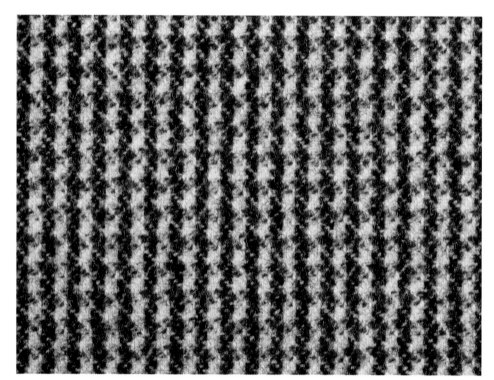

GUISACHAN

The old estate of Guisachan has now been broken up and sold largely to the Forestry Commission. It lies twenty miles west of Drumnadrochit on the Caledonian Canal and was originally part of the lands of the Frasers. In 1854 it was bought by Lord Tweedmouth who made extensive improvements to the lodge and estate and entertained King George V there. In the 1930s the estate was sold and Mr Donald Fraser now owns the Home Farm and house. The Guisachan tweed was first invoiced by Johnstons to Macdougalls of Inverness on 15th August, 1861 but it is now no longer used on the estate.

INGE

The Inge probably originated in the Elgin mills of Johnstons of Elgin and the first record of it was in September 1846. There does not seem to have been an estate of this name and it is impossible to trace its antecedents. About that time Affric was leased to a Colonel Inge and one can only speculate that the pattern was used for his stalkers. However it was made so frequently in the 1850s and '60s that Macdougalls must have sold it to all and sundry. The unusual red-brown colour, known in the mill as the Ing Drab, occurs in other tweeds.

INNES

Innes House is one of the finest seventeenth century houses in Scotland and was built by Sir Robert Innes of that Ilk in 1640. The house is a few miles east of Elgin in Morayshire. The house and estate were owned by Sir Iain Tennant, KT, but he has now made them over to his son Mr Mark Tennant. The tweed was made as long ago as 1872 as there is a note from Christie & Son of Edinburgh to Johnstons of Elgin, dated 17th April asking for a delivery date. It is now made for Sir Iain Tennant by Hunters of Brora.

INVERCAULD

The estate of Invercauld lies on the River Dee close to Balmoral a short distance east of Braemar and belongs to the Farquharson family trust. Captain A A C Farquharson thinks that the tweed was probably introduced by his great-grandfather Colonel James Ross Farquharson in the late 1800s. Johnstons of Elgin certainly made the pattern in the 1870s as it appears in one of the old pattern books. At that time the general tone was much less brown and the green overcheck much darker but there has been no change in the basic pattern.

INVERAILORT

The estate lies twenty-five miles west of Fort William and belongs to the Maclaren family. It has been owned by them for many years and has only changed hands once in the last six hundred years. During the last war the estate was requisitioned by the Navy and was the centre for Commando training. The original tweed design is taken from an old-fashioned automobile cap as was worn in the early days of motoring. It was the original tweed of the estate. The other design by Hunters of Brora has been used for the last five years. It is not unlike the Green Mar at first sight but the overchecking comes on every bass of the 4 and 4 section and the glen check is varied by using the basket effect on the 2 and 2 section. The estate is now considering readopting the original pattern which is extremely attractive.

INVERAILORT (ORIGINAL DESIGN)

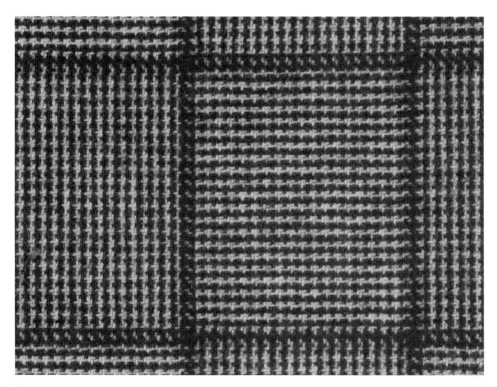

This is a handsome and simple design which has been on the books of Johnstons of Elgin for well over a hundred and twenty years. The origin of the design is lost and curiously enough neither Mr Angus MacIntyre of the well-known tweed warehouse in Inveraray, nor his father, had any knowledge of the pattern when it was illustrated in the first edition of this book.

INVERARAY

In the late 1940s Mr Michael Noble, later Lord Glenkinglass, gave this pattern to Mr MacIntyre as the Inveraray with the request that he get a length made up. Mr MacIntyre had it made by Alexanders of Peterhead from whom this sample came but I have no information on its antecedents, nor has the estate.

INVERARAY (GLENKINGLASS DESIGN)

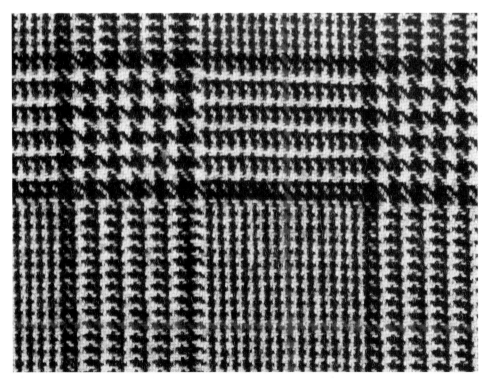

Invermark is one of the estates owned by the Earl of Dalhousie and lies west of Montrose in Glenesk (see page 113). The estate now uses the Dalhousie tweed but formerly used this striking Glenurquhart with its two thread scarlet overcheck on the 2 and 2 section. The repeat which is not very obvious in the illustration is about nine centimetres. Nothing is known of the designer nor when it was introduced but there is a possibility that it was once woven with a basket effect on the 2 and 2 section.

INVERMARK

The Islay Estates Company owns some 55,000 acres in Central and North-West Islay. It is owned by the Morrison family whose head is Lord Margadale of Islay, formerly Major John G Morrison. It is believed that the tweed was introduced in the early 1900s and, as it was made at the local Islay Woollen Mill, it was probably designed by Mr J T Christie who had the lease of the mills at that time. Back in the 1850s most of the island was owned by James Morrison and the estate has belonged to the family ever since. The tweed is also used on the family estates in Wiltshire.

ISLAY ESTATES

Kilchoan is a west coast estate and lies five miles to the east of Mallaig in the area of Loch Nevis. The estate was bought from the Knoydart Peninsula Limited by Mr Eric Delwart who designed the tweed with Hunters of Brora and introduced it in 1988. The makers of the tweed have now changed and the red and yellow stripes are slightly wider apart.

KILCHOAN

.The estate is on the Isle of Mull and is owned by Mr David Holman. The tweed was designed and introduced by Michael and Andrew Holman in 1992 with the help of the artists Brian Rawling and John Wonnacott. The design is a little unusual in its system of overchecks.

KILFINICHEN AND TIRORAN

The estate of Killiechassie lies about seven miles east of Aberfeldy in Perthshire and presently belongs to Robin Properties. The tweed was designed in 1955 by the late Group-Captain Hanchet-Taylor who then owned the estate. The tweed is now no longer used on the estate. The heathery ground colour is a little unusual and it seems to be based on a tartan design.

KILLIECHASSIE

The estate is beside the old British Aluminium Plant at Kinlochleven and is now owned by Alcan Highland Industries. It is administered by the West Highlands Estate office in Fort William. This tweed was first made for Sir Ian Walker and then Captain Reid-Walker of Ben Alder by Henry Ballantyne & Co of Walkerburn and was then transferred to the Killiechonate estate. The tweed has been woven at various times by Nobles of Hawick (now Peebles) and Hunters of Brora and the colours may have varied

KILLIECHONATE

The estate lies fifteen miles south-west of Perth beside Auchterarder and belongs to Mr Robert McNeil. In the 13th century the lands were granted to the Grahams, later the Dukes of Montrose. For thirty years from 1770 the estate belonged to Campbell of Glenure and it then passed to William Johnston at the beginning of the nineteenth century. It was acquired by Mr McNeil from Mr J Armstrong and the tweed was designed by Mrs Jayne McNeil and introduced to the estate in 1994.

KINCARDINE CASTLE

Kingairloch lies on Loch Linnhe a little to the north-east of the Isle of Mull and belongs to Mrs P Strutt. There was an earlier tweed than the one illustrated but its details have been lost and this one was introduced by Mrs Strutt in 1980 from a design by Hunters of Brora. It is now used on the estate.

KINGAIRLOCH

Kinloch estate is in the extreme north of Scotland and runs about fifteen miles south from the north coast down the Kyle of Tongue towards Altnaharra. It is owned by Mr A W G Sykes. The tweed was designed in 1986 by Mr Sykes helped by his wife Nicola and his aunt, Lady Simon. They used the dominant local colours to produce a good camouflage for the rugged terrain of the area which rises from sea level to over 3000 feet at the top of Ben Hope. The estate was purchased from Captain Charles Moncrieff whose family had owned it since 1936.

KINLOCH

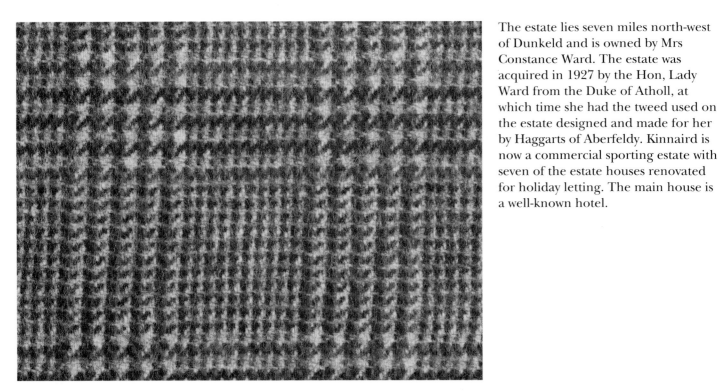

The estate lies seven miles north-west of Dunkeld and is owned by Mrs Constance Ward. The estate was acquired in 1927 by the Hon, Lady Ward from the Duke of Atholl, at which time she had the tweed used on the estate designed and made for her by Haggarts of Aberfeldy. Kinnaird is now a commercial sporting estate with seven of the estate houses renovated for holiday letting. The main house is a well-known hotel.

KINNAIRD AND BALNAGUARD

KINLOCHEWE

The estate of Kinlochewe lies at the southern end of Loch Maree and is owned by Mr Pat Wilson who bought it in 1993 from the Whitbread family. The estate has both a Shepherd check and Glenurquhart design which is rare. There is no information on who designed the tweeds or when they were created but Mr Wilson does not use them on the estate at present although he may do so in the future.

KINLOCHEWE (GLENURQUHART)

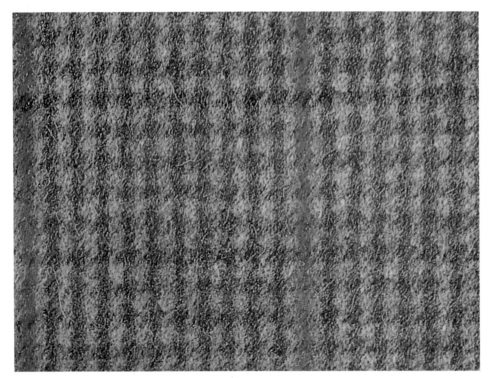

Kinnell is near Killin in Perthshire just south of the western end of Loch Tay. Since 1823 the estate has consisted of Kinnell and Auchmore. It used to be owned by J C Macnab of Macnab who designed and introduced the tweed in 1956 with the help of Haggarts of Aberfeldy. The estate has since been broken up. The hill has been given over to forestry and the house and policies are now owned by Group Captain Dowling.

KINNELL

The estate is twenty-two miles north of Dundee near Kirriemuir and is owned by The Rt Hon, The Lord Lyell. The tweed was designed by Campbells of Beauly and Lord Lyell's father about 1937. It is a variant of the Shepherd check, having a green line in the dark colour. Kinnordy was the home of the eminent geologist Sir Charles Lyell who died in 1875.

KINNORDY

Kinpurnie is fifteen miles south-west of Forfar in Angus and belongs to Sir James A Cayzer, Bt. He designed and introduced the tweed about 1980. It is a pleasantly simple design which provides good camouflage for the wearer. The twist of the warp marl produces a slight but noticeable diagonal effect.

KINPURNIE

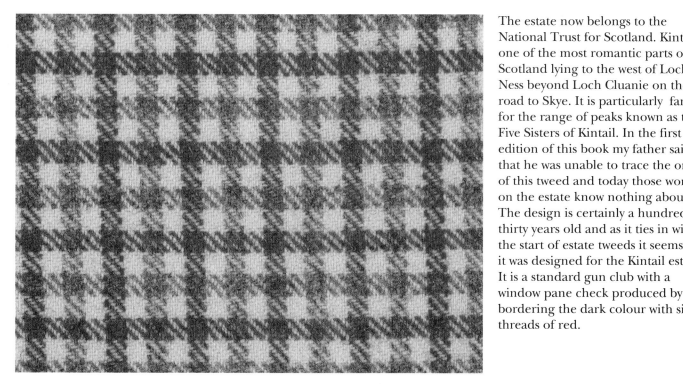

The estate now belongs to the National Trust for Scotland. Kintail is one of the most romantic parts of Scotland lying to the west of Loch Ness beyond Loch Cluanie on the road to Skye. It is particularly famous for the range of peaks known as the Five Sisters of Kintail. In the first edition of this book my father said that he was unable to trace the origins of this tweed and today those working on the estate know nothing about it. The design is certainly a hundred and thirty years old and as it ties in with the start of estate tweeds it seems that it was designed for the Kintail estate. It is a standard gun club with a window pane check produced by bordering the dark colour with single threads of red.

KINTAIL

KNOCKANDO

KNOCKANDO (GUN CLUB)

The estate is sixteen miles south of Elgin and is the property of Dr Catherine Wills, daughter of Sir David Wills, who bought the estate in the 1960s in two stages from Major Whitelaw who owned it in 1945. Before that the lands had been owned by the Grants. According to Sandy Milne the head ghillie, Major Whitelaw introduced the tweed just after 1945 and probably had it designed and made by Smiths of Knockando, the local mill. For two to three years in the 1970s Sir David used the second tweed, the gun club, but he then reverted to the original. The tweed is a straightforward Shepherd check, black in the weft and dark brown in the warp with a dark green overcheck of the same depth as the ground colours. The second pattern is a gun club, the moss-coloured weft check having two threads of green in it. Mr Milne says that when he came to the estate an old retired keeper told him that they used to use a brown herringbone tweed which would no doubt also have been made at the local mill.

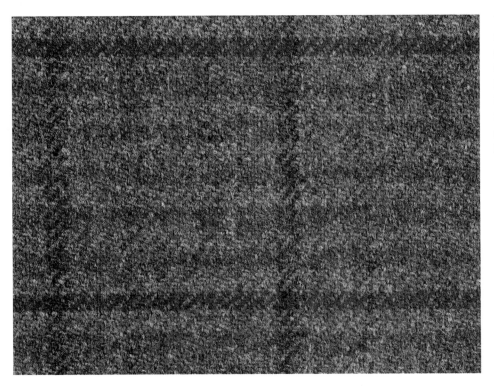

KNOCKDOLIAN

The Knockdolian tweed belongs to the Duke and Duchess of Wellington and is used on their estate near Colmonell in Ayrshire, the county of Robert Burns to the south-west of Glasgow. Properly the tweed belongs to the Duke's estates in Hampshire and it was designed by the Duke in the late 1940s for use on all his estates.

KYLNADROCHIT

Kylnadrochit is at Tomintoul in Banffshire, south of Elgin and belongs to Mr Jan Bolsius under the title Highland Sporting Estates Limited. The tweed was introduced in 1979 but the name of the designer, a local weaver, is not known.

LAIRG

The estate lies on the high ground above the dam on Loch Shin above the town of Lairg. It is owned by Mrs J R Greenwood. Originally the lands were part of the Sutherland estates but they were sold to Sir Edgar Horne in 1920 who in turn sold the estate to Colonel Leslie Bibby in 1960. Mrs Greenwood bought the estate in 1971 and J R Greenwood with Pringles of Inverness designed the tweed.

LAIRGIE

Lairgie is on the Mull of Kintyre just west of Arran and belongs to the Maxwell-Macdonald family. The shooting rights are leased by Mr John A Reid who uses a family tweed for this estate and also when he is the shooting tenant of other estates. The tweed was designed by Mr Covell of the Islay Woollen Mills in 1972.

The estate lies some six miles north-east of Ullapool and belongs to Mr A W Fenwick. The tweed was designed by Hunters of Brora and introduced to the estate in 1962. Until the end of the First World War the estate was part of the Cromarty lands. The design is a gun club on a Lovat ground and a quiet overcheck. The repeat is six centimetres.

LANGWELL

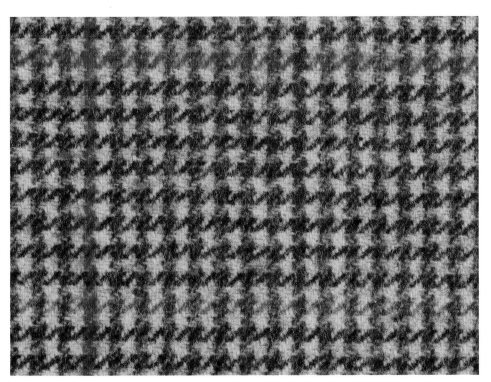

The estate of Laudale in Morvern in Argyllshire twenty miles north-west of Oban and was bought by the Abel Smith family in 1956. Mr Thomas Abel Smith adopted this pattern for his estate which was developed with Haggarts of Aberfeldy. The colours all have a symbolic meaning. The white and brown of the ground represent sheep and the mountains respectively, the blue on the overcheck is for the sea at Loch Sunart, the red is for sport and the green for the trees which they have planted on the estate.
The design is registered and is strictly confined to use by the family.

LAUDALE

The estate is two miles from the village of Comrie, twenty-five miles west of Perth, and is owned by Mr Robert Gibbons of Lawers. The tweed was designed by Mr Tom Simpson of Hunters and was introduced to the estate in 1973. The Mansion House on the estate was designed by Robert Adam.

LAWERS

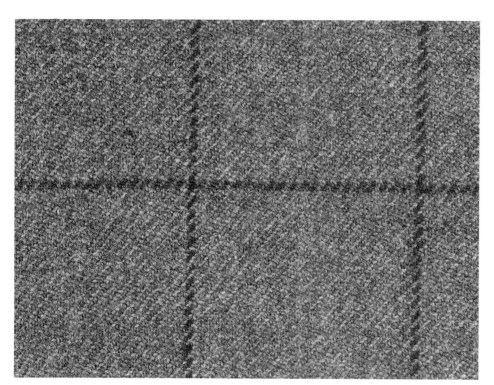

These two estates are both in Perthshire. Bandirran is eight miles north-east of Perth and Lochan about ten miles south-west of Dunkeld. They are both managed by Culfargie Estates Ltd which is owned by Sir Ian Lowson, Bt. He designed and introduced the tweed in 1990 and it is a little unusual in having a strong wine and green primary check and a very quiet secondary one in gold.

LOCHAN AND BANDIRRAN

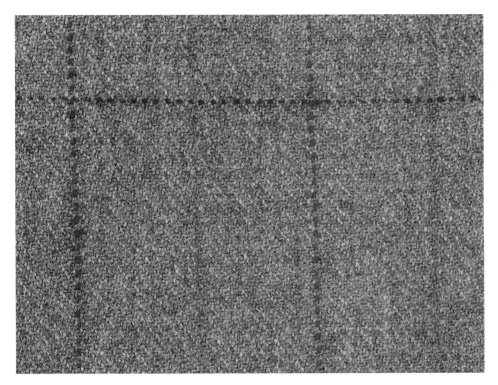

LETTEREWE

Letterewe is on the north side of Loch Maree and is owned by Mr Paul van Vlissingen who originally bought the Ardlair and Fisherfield portions in 1978. He designed a new tweed for those estates which is now used on the whole estate of Letterewe, the original tweed being discontinued. There are two version of the tweed, a gentleman's and a lady's. The original design was felt to be too loud but was reserved for the ladies and a quieter version was produced for the men. A length of tweed is presented to any lady who has spent a night at Carnmore, described as the third most remote house in Great Britain. The whole area is known as the last great wilderness. The men's version is illustrated along with the original tweed for which there are no details.

LETTEREWE (ORIGINAL DESIGN)

The estate of Achnacarry is at the south end of the Caledonian Canal near Fort William. It is owned by Sir Donald Cameron of Lochiel, KT. There are two slightly different versions of the estate tweed. The older was designed and introduced to the estate by Lochiel and Lady Hermione Cameron around 1906. The present design was introduced by Sir Donald Cameron of Lochiel. He modified the old design by introducing a grass green and Lovat mixture twist into the weft whereas before the same slack twist of grass green and fawn had been used in both warp and weft. The overchecking of scarlet and yellow remains the same in both designs.

LOCHIEL

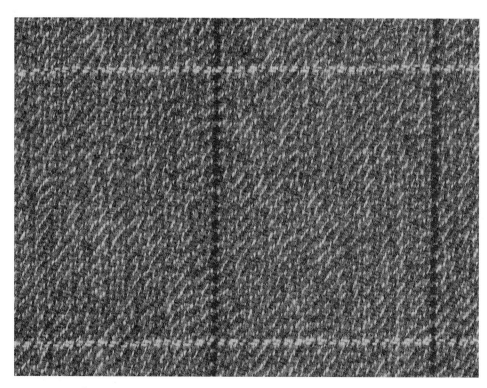

LOCHIEL (ORIGINAL DESIGN)

The estate lies at the south-east end of the Isle of Mull and from the 14th century to 1920 belonged to the Maclaines of Lochbuie who have their own tartan. It was bought by Sir Stephen Gatty and then by Sir Richard Garton in 1922, the grandfather of the present owner Mr John Corbett. The tweed was designed by Chalmers of Oban and introduced to the estate by Sir Richard about 1922. The green overcheck falls on every alternate bass of the 4 and 4.

LOCHBUIE

Lochmore is in north-west Sutherland about fifteen miles south-east of Laxford Bridge. It is part of the Reay Forest and is owned by the Westminster family. The tweed first appeared in one of the Johnstons pattern books over a hundred and twenty-five years ago but there is no record of its origin. It is an attractive form of the gun club or Coigach.

LOCHMORE

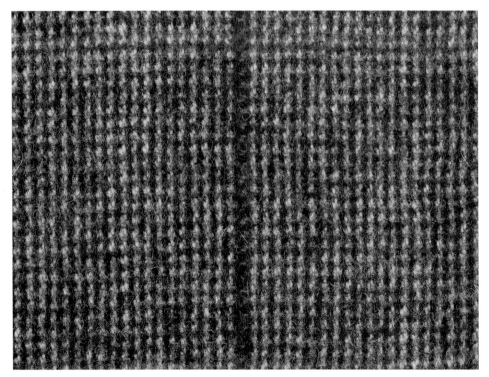

LOCHS

The estate is in Glen Lyon some fifteen miles south-west of Pitlochry. It belonged to Juliet, Lady Wills who used to live at Meggernie Castle and when she moved to Lochs she took the tweed with her. It was designed by her late husband Lt-Colonel Sir Edward Wills in the early 1920s. The estate was rented by his father during the First World War and then bought from Mr Bullough in 1919.(See also Meggernie, page 163).

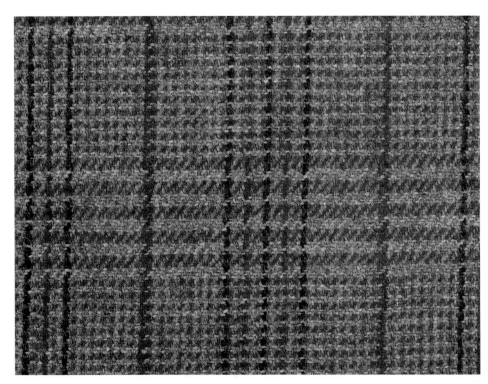

LOGIE BUCHAN

Logie Buchan is just east of Ellon, fifteen miles north of Aberdeen. It is owned by Mr and Mrs W H Bruce. The tweed was designed by Haggarts of Aberfeldy and introduced to the estate in 1993. The estate is unusual in being formed from a number of properties purchased during the period 1973–94 which reverses the general trend of big estates being broken up into smaller parts. Logie House which was built in 1976 was burnt down in 1993 but has now been rebuilt.

The Lothian estate lies round the Border town of Jedburgh about thirty miles south-west of Berwick. It is owned by the 11th Marquis of Lothian KCVO, DL and his family and the tweed is used on his estates. It was introduced some time before 1969 and was designed by Lord Lothian and Hunters of Brora. The basic design is a variation of the Shepherd check and the weft overcheck is so quiet that the overall effect is of a red warp stripe.

LOTHIAN

Lude is just two miles east of Blair Atholl and the other two estates are in Inverness-shire on the West Coast. All the estates are owned by the Gordon family and the design for the tweed was found in Inverness and introduced to Lude by Mr A D Gordon in 1930. It was used by Glen Quoich and Barrisdale when they were bought in 1956 and 1963 respectively.

LUDE, GLEN QUOICH AND BARRISDALE

THE LOVAT MIXTURE

The Lovat mixture is one of the first instances of protective colouring and is of great interest to Johnstons of Elgin as it was first woven in our mills. In 1968 Mr E S Harrison wrote: 'The present Lord Lovat tells me that he has been told that it was first designed by his grandfather for his keepers, ghillies and the family. As a small boy he heard that the idea for the colour came to his grandfather when looking across from the south side of Loch Morar. His grandfather pointed out to his grandmother how the contrasting colours of the primroses and bluebells which were in full bloom on the Letteir Morar side blended in with the hill, the white sands of the loch shore, the bracken and the birch trees. From that idea he mixed the tweed for its invisibility on the hill, which was an advantage for sport and deer stalking.' My father tried to trace its history because it was said that the first cloth had been woven at Newmill but without any success. Then by one of those unbelievable coincidences when he was in Canada he met an old wool man, Mr Fraser. Mr Fraser said that when he had been a boy he had worked at the Johnstons mills at Elgin. He remembered that Lord Lovat had consulted Mr Simon Fraser of Fraser and Smith, his father, who arranged that Johnstons should weave the cloth and after various trials the following mixture emerged as the original Lovat: light blue, thirty-eight parts; bright yellow, sixteen; chrome yellow, twenty-two; dark yellow-brown, twelve; white, twelve. Old Mr Fraser had kept a note of the original mixture although he had only the names and not the samples of the actual colours. These colours are an interesting and ingenious analysis of a Highland landscape on a bright spring day.

In the 1960s Mr Campbell of Campbells of Beauly recalled... 'my father telling me that my grandfather and the Lord Lovat of that period had some discussions as to the tweed which would be worn by the keepers of the Lovat estate. I do know that some kind of samples were run out, and were tried at Glen Strathfarrar to see how suitable they would be in matching the hill over which the stalkers would be working.'

The first piece was woven at Newmill on 26th September, 1845 and invoiced to Macdougalls of Inverness on 19th November as 'Lord Lovat's Mixture'.

Thereafter the name Lovat appears quite often in the Johnstons books.

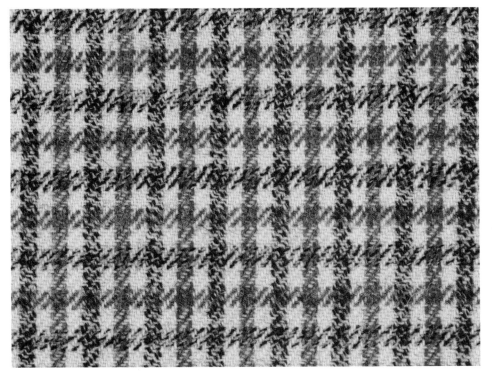

MAMORE

Mamore is at the head of Loch Leven about nine miles south of Fort William. In 1936 Mamore and the neighbouring estate of Killiechonate were bought by British Aluminium for the water rights for their smelter turbines. British Aluminium is now a subsidiary of British Alcan. Mr Andrew Brooks was the shooting tenant up to 1975 and Hunters of Brora designed the tweed for him then. It closely resembles a pattern called The Brook (page 105) which appears in a Johnston pattern book of the 1870s, but with no history. Mr Brooks says that the estate belonged to Mrs Cameron-Campbell in the mid-1800s and passed to the shipping family of Bibby at the turn of the century. It was sold by them in 1936.

MEGGERNIE

Meggernie Castle is in Glen Lyon twenty miles west of Aberfeldy. It was originally owned by Sir Ernest Wills, Bt who designed the tweed in 1920. It was made by Haggarts of Aberfeldy. The estate then passed to Lt-Colonel Sir Edward Wills, Bt but when he died his widow, Juliet, Lady Wills moved to Lochs taking the Meggernie tweed with her. Meggernie is now owned by Mrs J W Searle who introduced the new tweed shown here. The overchecking elements in both warp and weft are very quiet. It was also designed by Haggarts of Aberfeldy. In 1994 Meggernie was reunited with Lochs under Mrs Searle and the new Meggernie tweed continues in use on both estates.

MANSFIELD

The estate lies north of Perth on the east bank of the River Tay and is owned by The Rt Hon, The Earl of Mansfield. It has always belonged to his family. There are two versions of the estate tweed. The Glenurquhart check is used regularly on the estate and was designed and introduced by the late Dowager Countess of Mansfield and the present Countess of Mansfield about 1965. The other version was designed by the late Dowager Countess of Mansfield in 1949 and is worn by members of the family. It is woven from the wool of the Scone Palace flock of pedigree Jacob sheep which are bi-coloured with white and dark-brown wool. They can be seen in the Scone Palace park.

MANSFIELD (FAMILY TWEED)

THE GREEN MAR

THE RED MAR

Mar lies about ten miles south-west of Braemar and strictly speaking has three tweeds, the Green Mar, the Red Mar and a new version designed in 1990 which is not illustrated. The whole estate was originally owned by Captain Ramsay of Mar and it was split in 1960. Captain Ramsay kept the southern portion which is now in a trust administered by his son-in-law, Mr Mark Nicholson of Inverey House. It seems that before 1961 the family used to wear the Green Mar and the keepers and ghillies the Red but when the estate was divided the Ramsays retained the Green Mar for their estate, now called Mar. The Red Mar went to the north part of the Mar Lodge estate but is no longer in use. Tradition, not too well authenticated, has it that the Green Mar was designed by King Edward VII when, as Prince of Wales, he used to shoot from Abergeldie House in the Forest of Mar.

The design follows the Glenurquhart type with the alternate basses of the 4 and 4 part of the design being edged in dark green which is a little unusual. There is an entry in the old Johnstons invoice book to Macdougalls of Inverness for Marr (possibly a mis-spelling) in May 1870. At the time this book was being written, autumn 1994, the northern part of the estate, owned by Mr John Kluge with the new tweed design is up for sale.

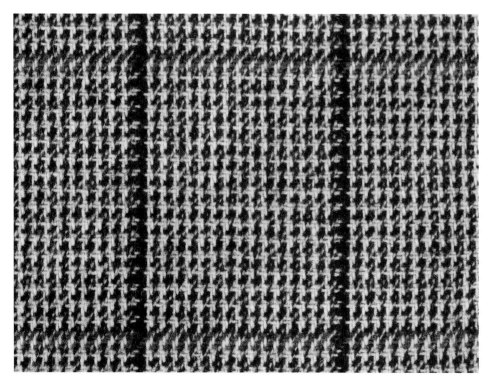

Millden is in the valley of the North Esk which runs five miles or so to the north of Brechin. It was bought from the Dalhousie Estates by Millden Estates Limited in 1987. The tweed was designed by Haggarts of Aberfeldy and was introduced to the estate, a famous grouse moor, in 1988.

MILLDEN

North Uist is in the Outer Hebrides and belongs to the North Uist Estates Trust 1990 who acquired it before 1967. There is no information on who designed the tweed nor when it was introduced to the estate.

NORTH UIST

Otter is on the Cowal Peninsula in Argyll twenty-five miles west of Glasgow. It is the property of Mr N K S Wills having previously belonged to the Rankin family. The tweed was designed by Haggarts of Aberfeldy and introduced to the estate in 1992. The overchecking on the moss-coloured ground is very quiet, two single orange threads in the warp and two single blue threads flanking a pair of moss-coloured threads in the weft.

OTTER

The estate is on the east side of the A9 road between Newtonmore and Dalwhinnie. It is the property of The Hon Michael J Samuel and the tweed was designed and introduced by The Hon Mrs P M Samuel.

PHONES

The estate lies in Strath Tay, ten miles north-west of Dunkeld and is owned by Tate and Lyle, the sugar company. It was bought in 1989 from the Kyd family. The tweed was designed and chosen by Lady Pixie Shaw, wife of the Chairman, following comments by the factor, Mr Macdonald, that many Scottish estates had their own distinctive tweeds, notably the neighbouring estate of Kinnaird.

PITCASTLE

Portmore is one of the Border estates and lies about ten miles north of Peebles. It is presently owned by Mr James Reid who bought it from Mr John Robertson. The estate has been unlucky in that Portmore House has twice been burned down, once in the 1860s and again in 1986. The tweed was introduced in 1993 and was designed by Haggarts of Aberfeldy.

PORTMORE

PITGAVENY

PITGAVENY (ORIGINAL DESIGN)

The estate lies three miles east of Elgin and belongs to Alexander Dunbar. It has been owned by the Brander and Dunbar families since 1765. The designer of the tweed is not known but the use of the Dunbar heraldic colours, gules and argent (red and white) on the overcheck suggests that Sir A H Dunbar, Bt, 1828–1910, had a hand in it. The design was probably introduced by Captain James Dunbar Brander who owned the estate from 1869 to 1902, when he was succeeded by his son Captain James Brander Dunbar, the original for John Buchan's *John Macnab*.

The ground colour varies from green to Lovat depending on the mixtures available at the mill making it and it is excellent camouflage in the Laigh of Moray or on the hill.

The second design illustrated is an example of an old pattern and shows how colours can change over the years. For many years the tweed was made by the Menzies mill in the village of Dallas in Moray, after which the great city of Dallas in Texas is named. But this mill closed down and the manufacture was transferred to Johnstons of Elgin who made the first design illustrated above. The change of colour due to a change of manufacturer is fairly common among estate tweeds but the change in the size of the overchecking is most unusual.

RALIA

The estate lies near Dalwhinnie on the west side of the A9 and is owned by Mrs Eira Drysdale. The tweed was designed by Hunters of Brora and introduced in 1985. The design is very unusual as it has a complex overchecking of blue and a group of four, two-thread orange-brown stripes with the strong twill herringboned in between them. The blue is checked with a quiet brown so that the overall effect is of a striped pattern. The repeat is eight centimetres.

REAY

Reay, like Lochmore, is in north-west Sutherland, twenty miles south- south-east of Cape Wrath. It is a large and desolate area owned by the Duke of Westminster. Like the Lochmore tweed there is no information on who designed this pattern nor when it was introduced but it is thought to have been selected by the 2nd Duke of Westminster some time after 1919.

ROTHIEMURCHUS

The estate lies just south of Aviemore and has been in the hands of the Grants of Rothiemurchus for many generations. There is no information available on the old tweed but the new one was designed by Haggarts of Aberfeldy and introduced by the present owner, John Grant of Rothiemurchus, DL in 1993. In the distant past the estate had various owners and in 1574 passed to Patrick Grant of Muckerach, son of the Chief of Grant. The high ground of the estate takes in some of the high tops of the Cairngorms and has been a National Nature Reserve since 1954. Elizabeth Grant's book *Memoirs of a Highland Lady* describes life on the estate in the early 1800s.

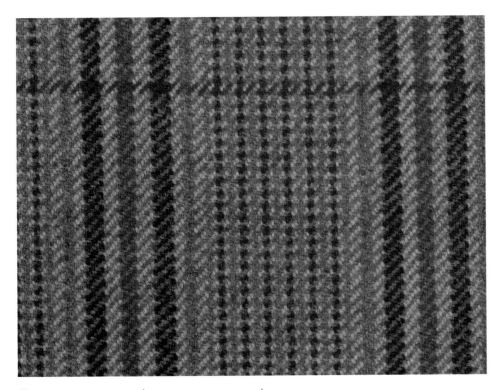

ROTHIEMURCHUS (ORIGINAL DESIGN)

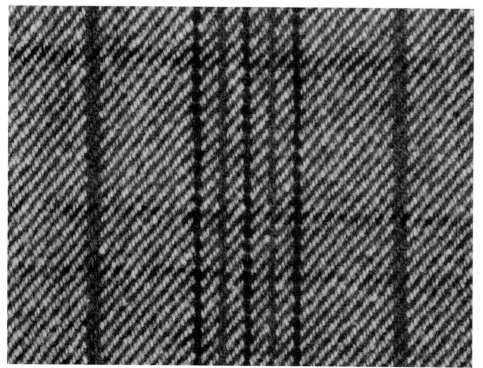

The estate lies in the north-east of the Isle of Arran in the estuary of the River Clyde and is the property of Mr C J G Fforde. The tweed was designed by Mr Fforde and introduced to the estate in 1975. Currently it is not in use. In between the double red lines in the weft and flanking them are two threads of a pinkish brown which tend to merge with the ground.

SANNOX

Scatwell lies in the glen of the River Conon about fifteen miles west of Muir of Ord in Ross-shire. It now belongs to Lord and Lady Guernsey under the title Packington Estate Enterprises Limited. The estate was purchased in 1990 from Mr Macdonald-Buchanan of Strathconon. Lord and Lady Guernsey designed a new tweed for the estate which is now known as Scatwell and Cabaan.

SCATWELL AND CABAAN

Loch Seaforth is on the east coast of the Isle of Lewis in the Outer Hebrides. There is no history of this design and it is really a Mackenzie tweed but it was adopted and used by the Seaforth Highlanders as a regimental tweed for the commissioned ranks of the regiment and presumably is still used by old members of the regiment. Perhaps this adoption is not surprising when one remembers that the regiment was raised by Kenneth Mackenzie, Earl of Seaforth. The pattern appears in the Johnston's pattern books of over a century ago. It is a beautiful scheme of two shades of brown on a white ground with a dull russet overcheck. The design is a standard gun club.

SEAFORTH

Strictly speaking the Shepherd check is not an estate tweed but, as it was the foundation of the first and many other estate tweed designs, it has been included as the first generic pattern. It is known the world over and is simply a small black and white check of about six threads of black and six of white. There is no definite standard. It was the traditional tweed of the Border shepherds and this was the design that Miss Balfour embellished with the scarlet overcheck to create the Glenfeshie mixture around 1840. It was said that Miss Balfour introduced this check to match the grey and red granite of Glenfeshie but another, possibly more likely version, has it that the purpose was to distinguish the men of the forest from the shepherds.

THE SHEPHERD CHECK

Skelpick is on the north coast of Scotland at Bettyhill in Strathnaver forty miles west of Thurso and belongs to the Lopes family. The tweed was designed and introduced by Helen, Lady Roborough in the 1950s.

SKELPICK AND RHIFAIL

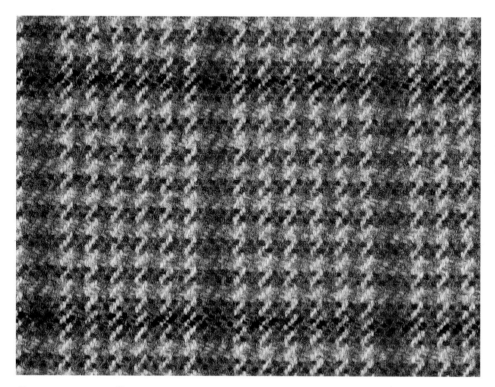

Snaigow estate lies a few miles east of Dunkeld and Glenquaich is about the same distance to the west. Both belong to Cadogan family interests. It is not known who designed the estate tweed but it was introduced by Lord Cadogan in the 1960s. It is a variation of the Shepherd check and deliberately covers the colour requirements of a low ground and moorland estate.

SNAIGOW AND GLENQUAICH

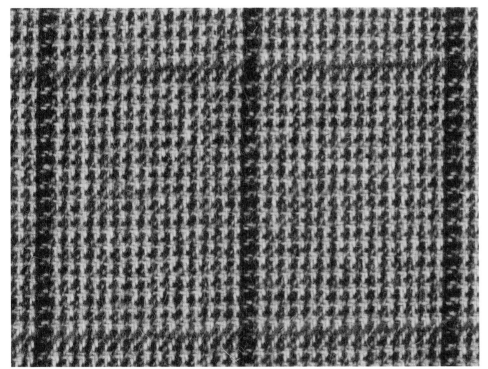

This is one of the Glen Lyon estates which lies to the west of Aberfeldy. It was originally part of the Campbell lands but then passed to the trustees of the Roy family from whom it was bought by the present owner Major-General C A Ramsay in 1978. The tweed was designed by Haggarts of Aberfeldy and introduced to the estate in 1980.

SOUTH CHESTHILL

As its name implies the estate is in the Outer Isles and belongs to the South Uist Estates Limited. The design of the tweed was most likely produced by Haggarts of Aberfeldy and introduced to the estate in 1960. The estate was previously owned by Lady Cathcart Gordon. Not very apparent in the illustration is a chrome-moss twist overcheck which is in the centre of the bass and also in between the three triple red warp lines.

SOUTH UIST

The estate lies a few miles to the south-west of Auchterarder and is the property of Sir William Denby Roberts, Bt. Before Sir William the estate belonged to Lord Perth but there is no information on who designed the tweed nor when it was introduced to the estate.

STRATHALLAN

The estate lies about twenty miles west south-west of Inverness and is owned by the Spencer-Nairn family. It was originally part of the Lovat estates and was sold to Colonel Cooper about 1920 and was then bought by Sir Robert Spencer-Nairn in 1934. When Sir Robert died his two sons inherited and the estate was divided in half along the line of the River Farrar. The northern half owned by Frank C Spencer-Nairn is called Culligran and the southern half still called Struy by Angus Spencer-Nairn. Both estates use the same tweed which has been worn on the estate since 1934 but there is no information on the designer nor the date of introduction.

STRUY

STRATHCONON

Strathconon lies in the area fifteen to twenty miles west of Muir of Ord. The estate was purchased by the Christiansen family from the Macdonald-Buchanans early in 1995. Before that it had belonged to the Combe family and before that Lord Balfour. The tweed now in use is the tweed designed by The Hon, Lady Macdonald-Buchanan for the neighbouring estate of Scatwell in 1953. When the Macdonald-Buchanans sold Scatwell to Lord and Lady Guernsey they retained the design of the Scatwell tweed for use on their Strathconon estates. Over the years the colours of this tweed have altered slightly and the present version is rather more yellow than the original. (See also Scatwell and Cabaan, page 172).

STRATHCONON (OLD DESIGN)

The original Strathconon tweed illustrated here is unusual as it is a plain diamond of eight by eight threads. Mr Peter Combe said that the tweed was introduced by his grandfather around 1909 but there is also a story that Lord Balfour who owned the estate before the Combe family dressed the troops of his regiment in the same tweed. The tweed was woven by the local weaver George MacIver in Dingwall High Street. Mr Combe has in his possession a collection of patterns of the tweed showing slight variations in shade and colour which he found amongst his grandfather's belongings. He said his grandfather sent his men up the hill carrying the tweed while he spyed them through his glass to see which pattern was the most invisible.

The estate lies on the Isle of Jura which is nearly cut in half by Loch Tarbert. It is the property of Viscount Astor who introduced the tweed to the estate in 1966. The weft element of the overcheck is not very obvious as it tends to sink into the ground.

TARBERT

The estate of Tillypronie is near Tarland in Aberdeenshire, thirty miles west of Aberdeen and is now owned by The Hon Philip Astor. The tweed was introduced by his father, The Hon Gavin Astor, who designed it in 1951. The general effect is of very dark heather. The overcheck on the warp is of two threads, one green representing the woods and yellow for the arable land, and in the weft the overcheck is a similar two threads, dark blue for the river and light blue for the sky on a herringboned ground.

TILLYPRONIE

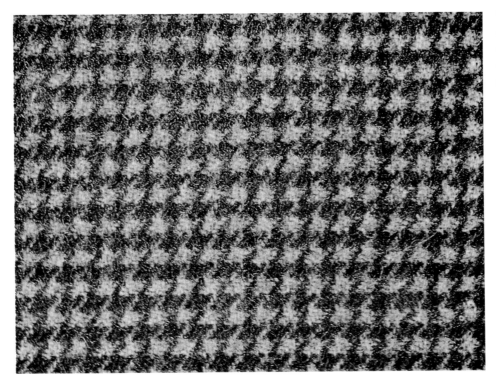

Tulchan is about nine miles north of Grantown-on-Spey and was once part of the Seafield lands. It has been owned by Mr and Mrs L Litchfield since October 1993. There is no information on who designed the estate tweed or when it was introduced but it is no longer in use on the estate.

TULCHAN

Urrard is two miles north-west of Pitlochry on the site of the Battle of Killiecrankie. It belongs to Mr Andrew Mackinnon who bought it from Mr Charles Findlay in 1988. The tweed was designed and introduced to the estate by Mr Mackinnon in 1989.

URRARD

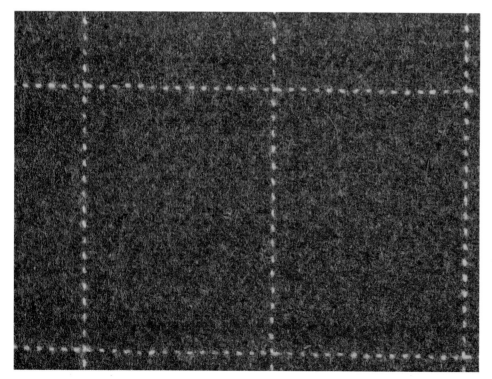

WEMYSS AND MARCH

The Wemyss and March estates, with lands in East Lothian, Peeblesshire, Selkirkshire and Gloucestershire are all administered by The Wemyss and March Estates Management Company Limited whose Chairman is Lord Neidpath, ARICS. The tweed is used throughout the estates in Scotland. It is a very simple pattern and the ground colour is very similar to the mixture produced for the London Scottish Regiment by Lord Elcho, who succeeded to the title of 10th Earl of Wemyss and March in 1883. The white check is very prominent and over-shadows the single thread of mid-blue alongside it.

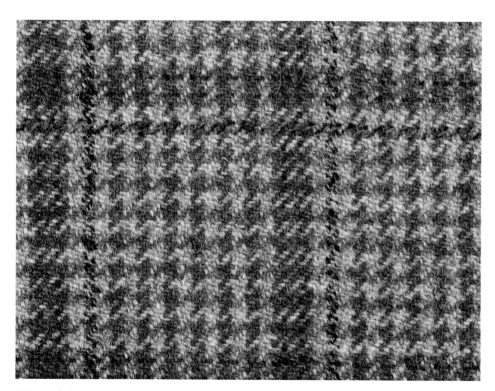

WEST MONAR AND PATT

The estate takes in the west end of Loch Monar which lies thirty-five miles or so due west from Inverness. It is owned by Mr C S R Stroyan who bought it from Captain R K W Stirling in 1965. The tweed was designed by Mr and Mrs Stroyan and Campbells of Beauly and has been used since 1966. The lodge at Patt is unusual as it can only be reached by boat down Loch Monar and is one of the most remote in Scotland.

WYVIS

Wyvis estate lies some fifteen miles north of Muir of Ord and is owned by Viscount Mountgarret. In the 1930s it was owned by the late Colonel Shoolbred who used the tweed on the estate. He believed that the tweed dated from the time the estate was bought by his uncle Walter Shoolbred in 1885 but the designer was not known. The present Lord Mountgarret's father bought the estate in 1981 and used his personal family tweed on the estate as the use of the original design had then lapsed.

The following estates are also believed to have their own tweeds but it has not been possible to get any details for illustration:

ABERCAIRNEY	HOPETOUN	POLTALLOCH
ANCASTER	INCHRORY	PORYARIE
BEN MORE	INNERWICK	REMONY
BLAIR CASTLE	INVERAN	RORO
BLACK CORRIES	INVERMERAN	STRATHMONESS
BRUCKLEY	KILMARONAIG	
CRAIGANOUR	KNOYDART	
DALLICK	LOCH DOCHART	
FINLARIG	LOGIE	
FORELAND	MINMORE	
GLENGLOY	MINTO	
GLENTROMIE	MONESS	
GORDON CASTLE	PITCARMICK	

A Glossary of
Spinning & Weaving Terms

A number of technical terms have been used throughout this book and this glossary has been included to explain them. Spinning and weaving are amongst the oldest crafts in the world, and however computer controlled and mechanised the modern weaving mill may be, the essential steps have remained the same for centuries.

FIBRE

The processes begin with the raw fibre and this can be divided into two main groups, wool and hair. Wool comes from sheep and hair mentioned in this book comes from cashmere goats, vicuna, camel, guanaco and alpaca. All animals produce differing qualities of fibre on the one fleece and before anything happens the fibre is sorted into coarse, medium and fine grades. This is done by hand to ensure that a standard quality of yarn can be spun and woven.

WOOL

The wool used for the estate tweeds came from North Country Cheviots, a breed of sheep introduced into the Highlands at the end of the 18th century.

DYEING

Dyeing can take place when the fibre is in its natural state or when it has been spun into yarn or woven into cloth. Dyeing requires dye powders, water, heat and agitation.

Before the end of the nineteenth century dyeing was done using natural materials such as bark, berries, seaweed, lichens and even insects. The old order books of Johnstons of Elgin contain many references to orders for the following dyestuffs: logwood for black, quercitron for yellow, sandalwood, madder and cochineal for red, ground redwood for brown, indigo and woad for blue, lacs from India for scarlet. The use of natural materials for dyeing produced a colour which

Cochineal beetles

Sorting cashmere by hand in Inner Mongolia

was not fast to light or abrasion and their inconsistent qualities made it very difficult for the dyer to reproduce the same colour exactly every time. This variation is no longer acceptable in the exacting markets of today.

The chemical dyes used today started as long ago as 1856 with the introduction of 'Perkins Mauve' the first of the anilene range. But it was not until the early years of the twentieth century that they came into general use enabling the dyer to produce an infinite palette of fast colours.

A modern dyehouse

TEAZING

Dyeing can leave the fibres in rather a felted and matted state and to open them and prepare for carding they are teazed out over a series of spiked rollers. At this stage the fibres are sprayed with a coating of light oil which protects them in the subsequent processes and makes them easier to manage.

BLENDING

Blends can be made of different colours of the same fibre or different types of fibre, eg cashmere and lambswool. The original Lovat mixture was created from a blend of light blue, bright yellow, dark yellow, brown and white. Such a blend in known as a 'mixture' and mixtures of this type are a traditional characteristic of Scottish textiles in general and estate tweeds in particular.

CARDING

After teazing the wool is fed into a hopper and from there it goes into a carding machine which mixes and straightens all the fibres preparatory to spinning. Carding converts a continuous web of fibres into individual ribbons of a speci-fied weight per unit length which can then be spun into yarn. These ribbons are known as rovings. It is an age-old process and has changed so little that one of the carding machines bought by James Johnston for his mills at Elgin in 1868 was still working satisfactorily up to 1993 when it was finally replaced.

SPINNING

Rovings are then converted into yarn by spinning. Spinning, twisting the fibres together to give them strength is carried out in two ways, on a mule which is the direct descendant of Arkwright's famous Spinning Jenny, or on a ring spinning frame. The thickness of the yarn is decided at this stage by drawing the rovings out to a pre-determined degree. Many different regional systems of measurement of yarn thickness were developed in the early years of the British textile industry and most of these still exist today. The term 'Galashiels cut' is one of these and refers to the length of yarn per 24 oz. Nowadays the thickness is mea-sured metrically.

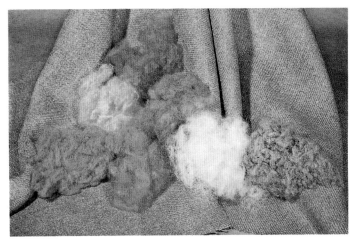

The original Lovat mixture showing the wools and woven tweed

Above: Carding – Scotch feed   Below: Mule Spinning

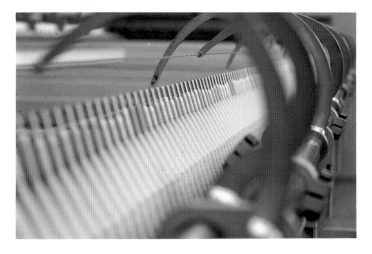

Above left: Ring spinning

Top right: Mule spinning, the modern version of Arkwright's Spinning Jenny

WINDING

When the yarn has been spun it is checked for regularity and wound onto cones. For some purposes it is preferable to have two-ply yarn where two single yarns are twisted together and then steamed to set the twist.

The Yarn Store

WARPING

Weaving starts with laying out the warp of the pattern. The warp is the threads which run vertically from top to bottom of the cloth. They are set out in a pre-determined colour pattern which is created by the designer. The number of threads in a warp varies according to the fineness of the yarn and the density and width of the fabric required. Warping was originally carried out by hand on warping stakes, a process which is still sometimes used for short sample lengths and design blankets. For production runs the warp yarns are wound from cones onto warp mills in the pre-determined colour sequence.

Top: Stake warping

Centre: A computer controlled pattern and sample length warp

Bottom: Mill warping

DRAWING

Each thread is drawn through a small eyelet called a heddle. The heddles are positioned on shafts in the loom which can be lifted and lowered in an infinite number of ways to form a variety of woven patterns *(right)*.

SLEYING

After drawing the warp passes through a wire reed which spaces the threads evenly across the cloth *(right)*.

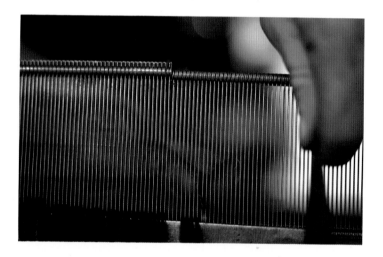

WEAVING

When the warp is ready it is then wound onto a circular beam and transferred to the loom for weaving. The weave is the introduction of the weft yarn, the threads that run horizontally across the cloth. The weft of a pattern, like the warp, is laid out on a pre-determined plan by the designer.

Various terms connected with weaving are familiar to everyone. The 'shuttle' is the device that carries the weft threads across the warp, the 'pick' is the action of throwing the shuttle across the warp and the speed and efficiency of a loom is measured in picks per minute. The 'loom' is the machine on which weaving takes place – a traditional broadloom was about six feet wide and a narrow loom about three feet. A handloom was operated by hand. Modern rapier insertion looms transfer the weft threads in the middle of the warp and they are both faster and more efficient than the old fashioned power looms.

Below: A pattern loom

TYPES OF WEAVE

There are various types of weave which depend on the manner in which the warp threads are raised and lowered in the weaving process. The simplest of all is plain weave. Scottish estate tweeds were very often laid out with the colour of the warp thread in groups of four, hence the expression 4 and 4. The twill or 'tweel' appearance, when the threads appear to run diagonally across the cloth, is created when the warp threads are raised two at a time, in sequence. In 'common twill', also known as 2 and 2 twill, the warp threads would be raised, one and two, then two and three, three and four, four and one. The sequence would then start again. The weft thread would consequently pass over and under two threads of the warp in each pass. If the designer wants to create a *herringbone* effect then the sequence of raising and lowering the warp threads is reversed.

The weaving shed

Plain weave   *Common twill*

Nowadays the diagonal twill normally runs bottom left to top right. This is known as 'twill right'. Many Scottish estate tweeds were however woven 'twill left' and this can be seen in the older patterns in the book.

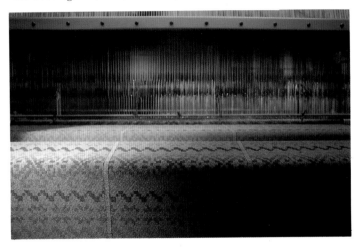

A Jacquard loom

THE GLENURQUHART DESIGN
The Glenurquhart design, also known as a glen check, which occurs frequently among estate tweeds is a simple pattern of a bass (an area of colour) of four threads of black alternating with four threads of white – 4 and 4. This is followed by an equal area of the same colours , two threads and two threads – 2 and 2. The arrangement is the same for both warp and weft and results in the warp striping effect on the 2 and 2 bass. By changing the sequence in which the threads are raised this warp stripe is changed to a weft stripe and this is known as the *basket effect*. The Inveraray tweed on page 143 is a good example of this.

JACQUARD LOOMS
Complex patterns can be created by varying the sequence in which the warp threads are raised and lowered and this is taken to the extreme by using a Jacquard loom where each warp thread is controlled individually. These were developed by Joseph Marie Jacquard in 1804 and are the forerunners of the modern computer.

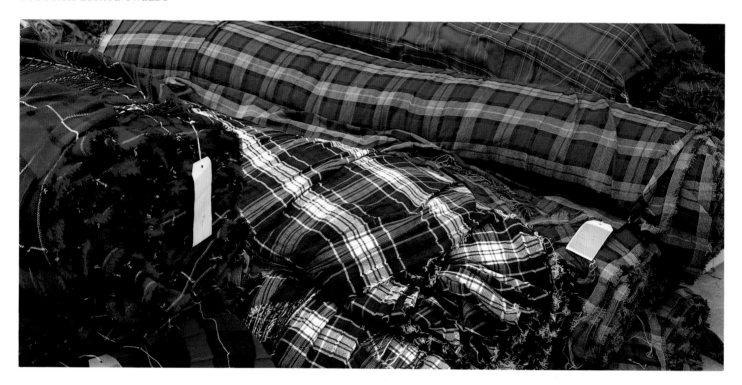

WET FINISHING

When cloth has been woven it is known as a web. Its appearance is rough and it then has to be 'finished'. This includes scouring, milling and raising.

Scouring

This removes all the oil, grease and dirt.

Milling

The fabric is shrunk and thickened, 'milled and felted', in a fulling mill. Originally this was done by stamping on the fabric in water from which came the old Scottish term 'waulking'. Nowadays this process is carried out by various types of machinery.

Raising

It is then raised by teazles or machine which plucks the fibres to the surface of the fabric. Teazles are used for cashmere which delicately teases and aligns the fibres to produce the characteristic ripple finish.

DRY FINISHING

After wet finishing the fabric is held out to a given width and then dried by passing it over heated rollers in a tentering machine. In the nineteenth century and earlier before machines were available fabric was hung up on hooks in the open air hence the expression 'to be on tenterhooks'.

Cropping

The cloth is then cropped by machines which act in the same way as a lawnmower to give the fabric a smooth, level finish.

Finally the fabric is inspected and pressed, packed and sold.

SCARVES

Scarves require additional finishing and are purled to create the fringe and slit on a machine and are then often embroidered and labelled before packing.

Above: Loom state webs

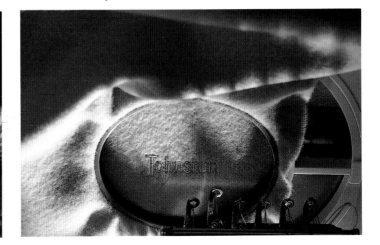

Top: Scouring   Centre: Teazle raising

Below: Tenterhooks

Top: Scarf purling   Centre: Scarf cutting

Below: Embroidery

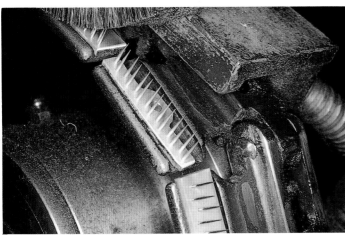

The mill shop at Johnstons of Elgin

Old Terms Used in this Book

A modern spinning and weaving factory has done away with some of the old processes which are referred to in this book particularly in the history of Johnstons of Elgin. Among the old terms some of which are still in use are:

'scribbling' which refers to the first stage of the carding process, the first part of a carding machine is still referred to as a *'scribbler'*;

'slobbing' or *'slubbing'* which was an intermediary process between carding and the production of rovings. Modern carding machines have a condenser which converts the fibre into ribbons (*rovings*).

Before this was invented this was done by a *'slubbing billy'* and the ends of the wool coming from the carding machines had to be pieced together by a *'piecer'*.

This was a boring and dangerous task and was often done by children before the introduction of factory legislation.

Other terms which need explaining are:

'homespun' which originally meant just what it said, wool sorted, carded and spun at home, came to mean a rough tweed with all the irregularities of hand spinning;

'twist' means two yarns twisted together to give an added colour dimension to the tweed;

'ground' is the basic colour of the tweed;

'bass' is an area of colour;

'overcheck' is the colour imposed over the basic pattern;

'a diamond' weave is when one herringbone is matched up with another in the warp.

CAPE W

ISLE OF LEWIS

Lochinver

Coigach

Ullapool
R.Oykell

Gairloch

NORTH UIST

Bonar Bridge
Loch Maree

Kinlochewe

R.Conon Din

Muir of Ord Be

Glen Strath
Farrar

SOUTH UIST

ISLE OF SKYE

IN

Cannich
Affric

Glen Moriston
Fort Augustus
Cluanie

Loch Nes

Loch Ne

Mallaig

Knoydart

Loch Oic
Loch Loch

Morar

Glenfinnan

TIREE

COLL

Ardnamurchan

Fort William
Kinlochleven

Glencoe

Rannoch

Aberfe

Loch Tay

ISLAND of MULL

Oban

Inveraray

ISLAND of JURA

Loch Lomond

Stir

ISLAY

GLASGO

ATLANTIC
OCEAN

MULL of KINTYRE

ISLAND of
ARRAN

Maybole

Girvan

NORTH CHANNEL